Japanese Workplaces in Transition

Also By Hendrik Meyer-Ohle

INNOVATION AND DYNAMICS IN JAPANESE RETAILING:
From Techniques to Formats to Systems

Japanese Workplaces in Transition

Employee Perceptions

Hendrik Meyer-Ohle

First published 2009 by
PALGRAVE MACMILLAN

Palgrave Macmillan in the UK is an imprint of Macmillan Publishers Limited,
registered in England, company number 785998, of Houndmills, Basingstoke,
Hampshire RG21 6XS.

Palgrave Macmillan in the US is a division of St Martin's Press LLC,
175 Fifth Avenue, New York, NY 10010.

Palgrave Macmillan is the global academic imprint of the above companies
and has companies and representatives throughout the world.

Palgrave® and Macmillan® are registered trademarks in the United States,
the United Kingdom, Europe and other countries.

ISBN-13: 978–0–230–22938–9 hardback
ISBN-10: 0–230–22938–7 hardback

This book is printed on paper suitable for recycling and made from fully
managed and sustained forest sources. Logging, pulping and manufacturing
processes are expected to conform to the environmental regulations of the
country of origin.

A catalogue record for this book is available from the British Library.

A catalog record for this book is available from the Library of Congress.

10 9 8 7 6 5 4 3 2 1
18 17 16 15 14 13 12 11 10 09

Printed and bound in Great Britain by
CPI Antony Rowe, Chippenham and Eastbourne

Contents

List of Tables

List of Charts

Preface and Acknowledgements

This book deals with changes in Japanese companies and labor markets during the prolonged aftermath of the bursting of Japan's bubble economy of the late 1980s and early 1990s. The following period – termed by some as a lost decade for Japan's economy – has led to significant changes in the way that Japanese people are employed and think about work. With the economy picking up somewhat again from the year 2005 onwards many onlookers have reckoned that the worst for Japan was over and it was time to consolidate, making sure that some of the profits that companies were making again found their way to employees or that working conditions and social security of the large contingent workforce that had built up were at least somewhat improved. Yet, at the time when the final steps on this book were made, the world was in economic crisis again, companies again talking about the need to reorganize and to reduce workforces, and policy makers being preoccupied with other issues. Already some onlookers are talking about the possible emergence of a second lost generation, a term coined to describe the situation of people who could only find work in the contingent workforce after companies restricted or changed their hiring policies.

Many people and institutions have helped to make this book possible and deserve credit. First of all, my colleagues and friends in the Department of Japanese Studies and the Faculty of Arts and Social Sciences at the National University of Singapore. The National University of Singapore (NUS) has also supported this book through its Academic Research Fund. A generous invitation to the Japanese Institute for Labor Policy and Training has enabled me to collect materials in Japan and discuss my ideas with colleagues at the Institute. The Asia Research Institute of NUS has provided me with a half year writing fellowship away from teaching and administrative obligations. Final revisions to the manuscript were made during a one year sabbatical at the College of Business Administration of Ritsumeikan University.

I would also like to thank the Japanese Institute of Labor Policy and Training, Recruit Corporation's Works Institute and the Institute of Labor Administration for their kind permission to use data, graphs and tables from their publications.

Individually I would like to thank Junko and Katsuhiko Hirasawa who have always helped me tremendously with my research in Japan. Student research assistants have helped with data collection and preliminary translation of Japanese materials and here I would like to thank Lee Wui Zhiang, Tan Bee Kee, Nai Mun, and Xie Quiaoguang. Christopher Kennard of Anchor English has provided proofreading services. At Palgrave Macmillan I would like to thank Virginia Thorp and Paul Milner for their support. Of course, all remaining mistakes are mine.

I would also like to thank my family for having supported me in writing this book. During our recent one year stay in Kyoto we have renewed our shared fascination for Japan and all things Japanese far beyond just matters of business and economy.

Finally, and most importantly, I would like to thank the writers of diaries on the Internet. I have used very small excerpts from many individual diaries, mostly just one part of one daily entry, weaving this into a new narrative to illustrate how Japanese people experience and think about changes at their workplaces. Yet, many of the individual excerpts stand out on their own, and while more subjective, might provide more memorable insights than much longer academic treatise on the same subject, thus actually inspiring the need for further research. Keeping a diary on the Internet is a laborious task and unfortunately some of the writers have by now discontinued their diaries, thus not all links that are provided in the back of this book still work. Many writers have also kept their identity anonymous and thus while every possible effort was made it was not possible to reach all writers. I would like to ask any writer who feels that changes are necessary to contact me and changes will be made in possible future editions of this book.

Kyoto, December 2008
Hendrik Meyer-Ohle

1
Changing Workplaces – Blogging about Work

1.1 Capturing change in workplaces

> *28 June 2001 – After work was finished we had a farewell party for early retirees. Because our company is in a slump, wages and bonuses have been cut, the coffers are in a desolate state. In this situation, a preferential early retirement system was introduced. When the company recruited retirees, quite a number of people raised their arms. Today was the farewell party for two of them. If such a number of people raise their hands, the future prospects of the company are surely bleak. But, if I retired, I would not be confident I could feed myself. I cannot retire.*[1]

The above citation is from the blog of a Japanese employee. Although just a short paragraph written in June 2001, it still provides information on the activities of a company, responses by its employees, speculations pertaining to the state of the company, and finally the problems of a single employee in coping with this situation. Thus the diary entry raises several questions: How typical of Japanese companies were and are the activities described? How do they relate to the overall situation of the Japanese economy? Are the feelings and speculations of this employee shared by others, and if so, how will this affect the future relationship between the company and employees in Japan?

The 1990s and beyond have been a period of intensive organizational change for Japanese corporations and their employees. Many companies that had supposedly outperformed global competitors through superior management techniques during the 1980s suddenly found themselves facing the need to review the way they were conducting business. Companies initiated changes in a number of areas, and human resources management was probably the area that received most attention.

Companies made significant changes that signaled a clear departure from what until then had been understood as Japanese management. Measures varied across industries and companies, but some core developments can be summarized. First, companies reduced the number of core regular employees through a variety of measures such as reducing the number of newly hired employees or by conducting voluntary early retirement exercises. Second, companies changed incentive systems by reducing the importance of seniority and increasing the emphasis on individual results. Third, companies significantly increased the number of non-regular employees.

Lifetime employment, advancement and remuneration by seniority, as well as the existence of company-based unions have been described as the pillars or treasures of Japanese management and as providing the foundation for a number of other features, such as long-term orientation of management, group work, bottom-up decision making, employee loyalty, continuous improvement and quality control or utilization of tacit knowledge. These features and behavioral patterns constituted what became commonly understood as Japanese management, and led Pucik and Hatvany to argue in 1980 that

> *the relationship between the organizational paradigm, strategies and techniques employed by management in many Japanese organizations is fairly complex. It is not a causal chain of policies leading to desired outcomes, but rather an integrated system that combines economic incentives and social control to achieve goal congruence on individual, group and organizational levels. It is also a reciprocal relationship: the employee's contribution to the organization is matched by providing him with economic security as well as by creating conditions for fulfillment of his emotional needs.* (Pucik and Hatvany 1980: 167)

Assuming management in Japan to be a set of highly interdependent features and behavioral patterns, with the employee or rather the employee-employer relationship being at the core, an understanding of the impact of the changes in human resources management on the perspectives and thinking of employees seems to be crucial for judging the changes that have happened since the 1990s.

However, this necessity is not restricted to Japan. Capelli (1999) in his influential study *The New Deal at Work, Managing the Market-Driven Workforce* paints a picture of the US of the past that resembles the popular image of Japanese employment patterns in many ways.

> *The old employment system of secure, lifetime jobs with predictable advancement and stable pay is dead. What killed it were changes in the way firms operate that brought markets inside the organization. In the process, labor markets were also brought inside the firm, and the pressures they create are systematically undermining the complex system of human resources practices that made long-term careers the staple of corporate life.* (Capelli 1999: 17)

Commenting on the changes initiated by employers he states that employees have reacted by becoming more interested in short-term gains from their current employment as well as in the long-term marketability of their skills. Consequently he argues:

> *While employers have quite clearly broken the old deal and its long-term commitments, they do not control the new deal, which is fundamentally an agreement negotiated between employer and employee. It is an open-ended relationship that is continually being redrafted. Which side gains and loses depends on bargaining power, which in turn stems from the state of the labor market.* (Capelli 1999: 17)

Capelli therefore provides us with a first intriguing reference point for the discussion of ongoing changes in Japan. How have Japanese employees reacted to corporate initiatives that in many regards seem to follow examples set by US companies earlier on? Will developments take a similar turn in Japan? Will employees become more independent and will there be consequences to what we have understood as Japanese management?

The consequences of changes in human resources management naturally go beyond the confines of managerial issues. Workplace conditions, relationships with superiors and colleagues, work security and satisfaction, career and life planning are all affected and therefore changes in employment practices can combine to lead to significant changes in the blueprint of a society. While probably true for most societies, it has been argued that for Japanese people, work has played a major role in shaping their identities, in addition to their understanding of society. Elements of Japanese employment such as long-term employment, remuneration and advancement by seniority, importance of educational institutions in recruitment, and comparatively low income differentials between labor and management certainly do not apply to all companies or employees but they have still contributed significantly to stability in Japanese society by providing people with strong normative points of orientation in regard to their past achievements, their own current position, or their own or their children's future ambitions. Overall, the real or perceived qualities of the Japanese employment system have contributed significantly to Japan understanding itself as a middle-class society with strong egalitarian and meritocratic elements.

Nohara argued in 1999 that structural change is taking place, though not in large sweeping moves but rather as the aggregated result of a number of micro-innovations.

> *Some of the institutional innovations constitute a direct assault on the most widely legitimated rules on which the Japanese model of HRM is based and are intended to create new patterns of behaviour among employees. Indeed, close observation of what is happening on the ground shows that the creation of new rules is being accompanied by innumerable attempts at mobilization involving the social partners or interactions between individual actors.* (Nohara 1999: 260)

Following Nohara's vocabulary this book attempts to take a close look at "what is and has been happening on the ground" and how this is leading to "mobilization" within the system. It will be shown that reforms which Nohara describes as "micro-innovations" have gained in weight and focus. It is still too early to identify the "clearly-defined, coherent whole" that Nohara asks for, however, having advanced several more years, directions of development have become somewhat clearer so that a first evaluation of the social and managerial consequences of the new developments can indeed be attempted.

This task has been made somewhat easier by the amount of information that has become available. Not only has the Internet allowed access to new sources of information such as blogs or Internet diaries by employees or online opinion surveys, but Japan's research institutions have also recognized the importance of the ongoing changes in labor markets and have consequently intensified their survey activities.

Thus, the objective of this book is to look into the recent and current developments in the management of human resources in Japan, with the aim of analyzing how these changes have affected the Japanese people in their workplaces and in their relationship with their employers. In doing this I look at three large areas. The first area concerns the restructuring of Japanese corporations. While restructuring is usually understood as a comprehensive process affecting all functions of the company, in Japan the term *risutora* [restructuring] has popularly become understood as solely meaning the reduction of the workforce. It is certainly not the first time that Japanese companies have reduced workforces, but during the 1990s this process went far beyond previous initiatives, affecting a large number of people across all industries. Companies came up with a number of different methods to reduce workforces and capacities, and it will be shown that restructuring efforts did not only affect employees who lost their jobs or left their companies but also affected those who stayed behind.

The second area concerns the so-called principles of Japanese management such as long-term employment, and advancement and remuneration by seniority. Since these principles are only sustainable in an environment where companies achieve long-term growth, pursuing these principles put a heavy strain on Japanese firms during the 1990s. Hence companies came up with various initiatives for change, changing working conditions not only for new but also for present employees. The main development here is the gradual replacement of age and capability-oriented principles of remuneration and advancement with result-oriented principles – a development that has the potential to change the way employees see their relationship with the company.

The third area concerns the diversification of employment and working patterns. The increasing importance of service industries, cost pressures, and a general trend to strive for a more flexible deployment of workforces have prompted company initiatives to significantly increase the ratio of employees who serve on limited rather than regular contracts, work shorter hours, receive pay by the hour, or are even employed indirectly through sub-contractors or staffing agencies. Non-regular or atypical work has not only increased quantitatively but has also changed qualitatively in as much that increasingly employers ask non-regular employees to perform more responsible tasks. Based on a number of factors on the supply as well as the demand side, for an increasing number of younger people atypical employment has become the norm, either by choice or by necessity, and this not only has consequences for the way companies are managed but also for the societal development of Japan in general.

The discussion of the three areas above largely determines the structure of this book. The following chapter looks at the development of human resources management from firms' perspectives. Companies changed human resources management from the 1990s onwards for different reasons and in different ways. This outline and discussion of corporate strategies sets the stage for the main part of this book, the initiatives in reorganization of human resources management as seen by employees. This part consists of three chapters that follow the above three strands of development, restructuring and redeployment of workforces, changes in the principles of human resources management, and finally the diversification of employment and working patterns. The concluding chapter considers the future of Japanese employment relationships and working patterns and also provides managerial and societal implications.

Before proceeding to the introduction of the sources I would like to make two additional introductory remarks. The first point is with regard to the degree of change that happened and is still happening in Japanese companies. While many elements of the so-called Japanese management system were for a long time seen in a largely positive light, a reminder is necessary that there was always awareness within Japan's corporate world of potential risks that came with the use of the various elements. Thus, the initiatives from the 1990s onwards were certainly not the first. In fact, companies have continuously made moves to incrementally reform the management of human resources. After all, what has come to constitute Japanese management has not always been around in its totality. Certain elements might have associations with Japanese tradition, but it is difficult to establish historical continuity. New elements were consciously introduced and what we finally came to understand as Japanese management during the 1970s and 1980s was fully established only during the 1960s.

Still, at the time of writing this book an agreement seems to have formed that change in the management of human resources from the 1990s onwards has gone far beyond the incremental adjustments of the past. Initiatives had and have disruptive qualities and are a clear break away from those paradigms that were understood inside and especially outside Japan to constitute Japanese management. This is especially so since change is not only driven by established firms reforming their existing employment practices to stay competitive. Change has also been driven by newer, less established companies, especially from the service sector or foreign companies. These firms have confronted existing models of employment with alternatives that demonstrate a highly flexible and cost efficient use of human resources based on innovations in incentive systems and a systematic diversification of employment patterns. Changes in human resources management practices also occur in relation to changes in the regulatory environment. Law makers and courts have on the one hand made moves to somewhat strengthen the position of older workers, female employees, or non-regular employees but on the other hand have also provided employees with more flexibility in employment practices, for example the possibility of employing dispatch workers across a widened spectrum of occupations. Finally, change has been driven by employees themselves. Not all employees were satisfied with an employment system that offered a high level of security but was at the same time mentally and physically very demanding in regard to working conditions and/or limited recognition of individual achievement.

Second, as already indicated, many developments outlined in this book reflect developments seen in other countries. The management of human resources and working conditions has undergone significant changes not only in Japan, but worldwide, and seen from the perspective of the majority of employees these changes might often not have been for the better. The blog entries and other sources will reveal the perceptions of Japanese employees, and often the reader might ask "Isn't that obvious, wouldn't anyone think and react like that?" or "Isn't the author just reinventing the wheel?" While provoking such questions can already be seen as a welcome result by itself in view of all the books written inside and outside Japan propagating Japanese exceptionalism, this book is not written from a comparative perspective. I would like to ask the reader to keep this point in mind and not to regard this book as an attempt to highlight developments in Japan in either an exceptionally positive or negative light. Rather I hope this book will be regarded as an interesting and thought-inspiring snapshot of the state and concerns of a society and economy in a challenging period of transition.

1.2   Blog entries to learn about employee perceptions

Diary writing has a long tradition in Japan. Some of the country's earliest pieces of literature were written in the form of diaries during the Heian Period 1,000 years ago, a tradition that continued throughout the centuries until today (Keene 1999, Varley 2000). Writing a diary is regarded as an important experience and most Japanese children are still encouraged to keep a regular diary during their middle school days (LeTendre 1994, Kawaura 2000). Donald Keene even speaks of a Japanese absorption with diaries (Keene 1999: 11). Clearly this fascination has extended to diary writing or blogging on the Internet, and it explains why Japan, which has otherwise been described as an Internet latecomer, saw Internet diary writing flourishing early on. Based on their popularity in Japan, conventional diaries have been used frequently by those in academia to gain insights into various issues (e.g., Keene 1995 or Sheldon 1976). Just the same, Internet diaries can be an attractive source.

The Internet provided a variety of results when looking for accounts related to restructuring and changes in workplaces and there was always a danger of getting lost in the process. In this regard it helped that many diary portals offered a search function and this function allowed searching across several diaries. However, finding ways to systematically access online diaries is only one of the issues that needed to be overcome, the main one being the ambiguity of results. In regard to reliability, online diary entries can be located between two extremes:

- Online diary entries as a tool for people to simply write about their own experiences, stating their opinions and perceptions spontaneously and in a setting not influenced by the researcher in any way.

* Online diary entries as fictional accounts that are written to entertain and to initiate communication with an audience of readers.

Of course, there is much middle ground between the two extremes. For example, writers might bring up an issue, not because it comes to their mind spontaneously, but because they have been exposed to the issue in the media and they feel that their own experiences are relevant to it. Thus it cannot be guaranteed that all accounts are close to reality or totally based on diary writers' perceptions alone. While some might argue that this is not an issue at all because even fictional accounts show actual concerns of writers and their audiences, some precautions were taken in this regard, mostly by trying to limit accounts used to those from non-themed diaries.

Just entering restructuring (*risutora*) and diary (*nikki*) in Japanese into Google Japan at www.google.co.jp returned 233,000 results. The first results that appear in this list linked to blogs that promised to deal exclusively with issues of restructuring. An example of this is a "New Restructuring Diary"[2] that outlines the experiences of an employee in the retail industry. In style and content such themed diaries are clearly written for a larger audience and authors, constantly under pressure to add new and interesting developments, may be tempted to come up with fictitious events. However, theme-based blogs form only a very small number of the overall number of diaries in Japan. Most diaries, even some that start with a main theme, cover a variety of topics and most are simple chronicles and perceptions of daily events and are thus usually rather trivial at first sight. Yet, it is especially these non-themed diaries that seem to be most reliable in terms of the information provided, so these were used in this book.

The second issue that involves some ambiguity is subjectivity. On the one hand, subjectivity is clearly the strength of online diaries. Blog writers state their feelings, opinions and perceptions freely. For example, when looking at workplace conditions and events, for the employee perceptions probably carry at least as much or even more weight than the supposedly objective state of things, for example the concrete design of incentive systems by one company in comparison to another company. Hence diaries can be considered an ideal source for perceptions that are expressed in a spontaneous way and in an unbiased setting. On the other hand, a single diary entry might only represent the isolated subjective view of a single employee and might therefore not be representative for any other employee, especially since blogs have been recognized as a means for people to deal with pressure or extraordinary events. As such there is a certain probability of bias towards the extraordinary.

There is a third point in regard to the sample used. Using diary excerpts leads to a certain self-selection of writers. While there is no gender bias there is a bias towards writers in their 20s and 30s. Yet, it is not exclusively those age groups any longer who are using the Internet to express themselves. Looking at the 125 diary entries introduced in this book, 74 entries were written by male authors and 47 by female authors (4 undetermined). Looking at age, for 65 writers the age could not be determined while from the rest, 26 were in their twenties and 24 in their thirties, 7 in their 40s, and 3 in their 50s.

Based on the considerations above the following methodology in regard to the use of diary entries was developed. First it was decided that diary entries could not be used in a quantitative way and that any method of applying quantitative methods would simply suggest an objectivity that does not exist. Second, the search for diary entries went through a process of refinement as the research progressed. In the early stages of the project diary entries were sought by entering certain keywords such as *early retirement (sōki taishoku), transfers (shukkō)* or *dispatch work (haken)* together with the word diary (*nikki*) into Japanese Google. This led to a high number of results that did not link to diaries but to web pages that just contained the terms searched for in another context. Therefore the search was later concentrated on diaries published in two of the leading diary portals (Saru Saru Nikki at http://diary.ne.jp and Diary Note at http://diarynote.jp). Both of these allow searches of their websites. The links were than accessed and daily entries that contained the relevant search terms were entered into a database together with available information on authors. Altogether, about 1,000 records were collected using this process. Records were then sorted by topic and for each topic the major sub-themes brought up by diary writers were identified. The identification of these major sub-themes was then used to sort diary entries into a new narrative that outlined diary writers' experiences, feelings and perceptions in regard to the various issues addressed in this book, for example voluntary early retirement exercises, performance-based incentive systems or dispatch work.

This new narrative was then contrasted with other sources, especially surveys of employees and company representatives. Often survey data supported opinions by blog writers and showed that experiences and opinions of diary writers were indeed shared. However, surveys also showed that certain perceptions only reflected minority views. Thus, survey results became a necessary resource for qualifying and complementing results of diary entries. Diary entries and survey results were then integrated into the discourse on management and work in Japan and beyond.

2
Japanese Corporations under Pressure: Changing Employment Practices in Three Industries

Japanese companies came under intense pressure to change employment practices from the 1990s onwards. These pressures and the companies' responses will be outlined by looking at three industries. The electronics industry represents Japan's manufacturing sector. Japan's electronics companies grew rapidly in the post-war period and managed to assume a leadership role despite intense worldwide competition before their position was threatened in the 1990s. The electronics industry uses employees in a wide variety of occupations, including the actual manufacturing process, research and development, and administration. However, it is the care that companies took in the employment of blue collar workers that has been particularly linked to Japan's strength in production efficiency and product quality. Banking represents white collar employment. Employees of financial institutions were seen as elite, with privileges in terms of remuneration levels and security of advancement. However, developments such as financial deregulation and the after effects of the bubble economy have driven Japan's financial sector into an ongoing period of reorganization. Finally, retailing represents consumer-oriented services with high customer expectations in terms of service quality and increasingly in terms of constant availability over space and time. By fulfilling these demands Japan's retail companies have become pioneers in the employment and management of a large contingent workforce.

2.1 Electronics industries

Towards the end of the 1980s Japan's Electronics Industry appeared to be invincible, having largely conquered world markets in major home electronics and appliances and also having captured large shares in other important areas such as the semiconductor industry. This situation changed in the 1990s when Japanese companies had to cope with a series of interrelated developments such as low profitability and falling market share of their semiconductor operations, drastically falling unit prices for household appliances and the modularization of products. For example, from 1990 (100) the wholesale price index for communication equipment dropped to 92.8 points in 1995 and further to 54 by 2002. Employment in the industry fell from 1.94 million employees in 1999 to 1.45 million in 2001.

The problems that most Japanese electronics manufacturers encountered from the 1990s onwards were mainly related to the broad spectrum of business activities they engaged in. Continuously competing for revenue growth and market share, firms were always quick to move into new areas, but unlike many Western competitors, they did not usually divest business ventures that showed decreasing returns. Striving for a lasting presence in every area, electronics manufacturers thus maintained large numbers of divisions and subsidiaries, among them many which were not competitive on their own. At the same time, American companies came up with the highly flexible new business model of modularization, which included a high degree of standardization of parts and the outsourcing of production processes (EIRD-DBJ 2002). Falling unit prices, the shift of production to overseas locations, depressed consumer and industrial demand as well as the activities of overseas competitors led to a rapid decrease in production values (Nihon Denki Kōgyōkai 2004).

Falling revenues and decreases in competitiveness pressured Japan's general electronic companies to review their operations, and companies came up with a number of strategies. The first included an increasing shift of production to overseas locations. From 1993 to 2002 the share of overseas production increased from 12.6% to 26.5% for the whole electronics industry, with single companies reaching levels that were substantially higher (KSS/KRS/MKS 2004). Another development was the consolidation of business activities, with companies retreating from some areas completely, scaling down capacity or deciding to consign manufacturing to other companies. Some units were spun-off or even merged with those of competitors. In this quest Fujitsu and Toshiba withdrew from the production of DRAM. Hitachi ended the production of components and devices for scanners and CRTs. Matsushita, Hitachi, NEC, Fujitsu and Mitsubishi closed some of their overseas factories. Mitsubishi outsourced the production of cellular phones and NEC did the same with the production of servers. Sony, NEC and most other companies turned some divisions into in-house companies. Finally Sony, Matsushita, and NEC divested some of their production divisions or increased their independence to serve the EMS (electronics manufacturing services) market (EIRD-DBJ 2002).

The pressures experienced by electronics manufacturers from the 1990s onwards resulted in changes in the management of human resources. The measures taken can be split roughly into three areas: a reduction in employee numbers, changes in the composition of workforces, and changes in employment conditions for regular employees.

Responding to over-capacity, the relocation of production overseas, the reorganization of production facilities in Japan and finally increases in the average age of their employees, Japanese electronics companies scaled back their workforces, the first move being cutting back on the hiring of new employees. While in the year 1992 manufacturing companies had recruited a total of 340,000 fresh graduates, they reduced this figure to only 179,000 by the year 2001. Here, large corporations with more than 1000 employees were the most thorough, reducing the number of fresh graduates hired from 134,000 to just 44,000 (KSS/KRS/MKS 2003).

In addition, firms also implemented early retirement strategies. One of the leaders in this regard became Matsushita, a company widely regarded as representing Japanese management principles in the strictest and most conservative way. In 2001, Matsushita conducted a massive early retirement exercise that saw 13,000 out of 100,000 eligible employees applying for the scheme and eventually retiring, 5,000 more than the company had originally targeted. Leading to a reduction of 4.4% of Matsushita's total workforce, the program was one of Japan's largest ever workforce reductions via early retirement. Targeting workers across all functions, 13% of retirees were engaged in administration, 14% in sales, and 60% in manufacturing. The remaining retirees came from technical development, among them 2% who were involved in pure development. In April 2002, Matsushita conducted another exercise that reduced its sales staff by 5,000 people (*NKS* 22 February 2002, *NSS* 12 July 2002). Other electronics manufacturers also conducted early retirement exercises. Hitachi received 9,000 applications when it announced in 2002 that it was recruiting 4,000 employees above 40 years of age and NEC recruited 5,000 employees for early retirement (*NKS-NNI* 8 April 2002, 5 August 2002).

Changes in the management of human resources went beyond simple adjustment of employment figures. Electronics manufacturers expressed their determination to keep a certain amount of production in Japan. These were high-value-added activities that were closely linked to research and development, but also included the production of goods with very short development and demand cycles. Thus, although overall production capacity clearly decreased in Japan, some Japanese companies such as Sharp, Fujitsu and Kenwood opened new factories in Japan.

Yet, within factories the composition of workforces has changed significantly. Instead of using regularly employed assembly workers, firms lease out parts of their factories and some of their manufacturing equipment to on-site sub-contractors or use contract workers (*NSS* 2 April 2004, *NKS* 23 December 2001, *NKS* 13 May 2004, *NKS* 1 April 2004). Subcontractors use production lines and facilities from manufacturers to produce for manufacturers and in theory supervise their own work crews. Thus, manufacturers enjoy substantial cost reductions. Labor costs per hour for a contract employee are estimated to be approximately 1,300 yen compared to 3,000 yen for regularly employed workers. In addition, manufacturers gain flexibility by being able to quickly adjust production levels as soon as new products are introduced.

During the 1990s the popularity of this method increased rapidly. Estimates put the number of people working for such on-site subcontractors at 1 million, out of a total of 12 million manufacturing employees. The union Denki Rengo estimated that 18% of workers in the electronics industry were employed and managed by on-site contract companies (*NSS* 14 April 2004). Canon alone uses 16,000 contract workers within its factories. The 800 workers in Japan's largest computer assembly facility owned by Fujitsu are nearly all contract employees.

Finally, electronics companies have been changing the way they manage their regular employees. Besides short-term measures aiming at immediate cost cuts, such as forced vacations or freezing regular pay increases, they have made significant efforts to move work and incentive patterns away from the relatively standardized patterns of the past that were based on seniority and long-term employment. Companies have introduced merit-based systems that allow for a stronger differentiation in remuneration and faster advancements within companies. In accordance with managerial needs and to reflect productivity and economic results, companies also laid the foundations to differentiate employment and incentive systems between different units and subsidiaries.

NEC has differentiated bonuses between employees of its various units and subsidiaries based on contributions to overall company results. NEC also introduced a system for its engineers to honor professional skills. The company had already introduced a system that designated certain employees as specialists in the early 1990s; however the system had not distinguished properly between the different employment categories. Despite being awarded their new status, specialists were still largely treated the same way as other employees. Under the new system, treatment became more flexible and allowed for higher rewards (*NSS* 12 April 2002). In 2002 NEC went a step further and introduced a grading system for all its 12,000 managerial employees. Employees were ranked into seven groups and detailed descriptions of performance expectations, responsibilities and necessary qualifications were made available to all employees by publishing them on the company's intranet (*NKS* 8 July 2002). NEC also began to link retirement allowances to achievements. In its software company, NEC reduced the seniority component used in the calculation of retirement allowances from 70% to 30% and increased the weight of the competence component accordingly. Employees now accumulate points for achievements, but the new system also reduces points should employees remain on the same level for too long (*NKS* 21 November 2002).

Other companies engaged in similar activities. In July 2001 Hitachi reached an agreement with its union that enabled it to differentiate treatment of employees between its various operational units and to introduce separate qualification and remuneration systems. Based on this agreement the company has introduced a new merit-based system in its telecommunications division. Here it grouped 7,000 employees into eight different occupations and four ranks. Top ranked employees were reported to earn significantly more than their colleagues (*NKS* 29 August 2001). Having done away with seniority-based remuneration for managerial employees in the year 2000 Hitachi announced the introduction of merit-based pay and the abolition of seniority elements for all of its 30,000 non-managerial workers from April 2004, a first among the large general electronics companies. The company came up with a complex ranking system to decide on base wages and will evaluate employees yearly to decide on wage increases or decreases and advancement opportunities. Previously, seniority-based elements had accounted for about 40% of wages (*NKS* 17 March 2002, 17 November 2003).

Other companies that announced they were doing away with seniority-based systems for administrative employees included Sony and Matsushita. In the case of Sony its move in 2004 also abolished all extra allowances, such as those for housing or married employees. Matsushita had initially excluded blue-collar workers from its reforms, but in 2003 announced plans to remove seniority components for all of its employees by early 2004 (*NKS* 1 July 2001, 29 November 2003, 26 November 2003).

While companies had kept employment conditions for newly hired school or university graduates mostly standardized, including regular wage increases, Sanyo in January 2004, in what was described as a first for the electronics industry, announced that it would differentiate pay for new hires, with wages for entry level employees possibly even exceeding those of employees with longer tenure. Two years earlier the same company had already begun to single out certain employees for elite development as soon as they were hired (*NKS* 3 April 2004, 16 January 2004).

2.2   Banking

The banking industry was the sector that was hit most directly by the burst of the bubble economy at the beginning of the 1990s, but it would be simplistic to relate the problems that Japan's financial sector experienced only to this event (Choy 1999). The burst of the bubble economy led to a general decrease in the value of assets of banks as well as their creditors. Largely following their standard approaches to dealing with problematic creditors, banks initially renegotiated terms, but due to the overall harsh economic environment many creditors could not fulfill their obligations, which led to an accumulation of so-called bad loans. This situation was initially not dealt with decisively by either banks or regulators.

In addition, banks were faced with deregulation, mainly the abolition of rules that clearly assigned certain transactions to specialized financial institutions, a liberalization process that had been initiated in the early 1980s. While providing new opportunities for some, for others the change of rules took away assured business. Banks looking for new sources of income provided more resources directly to domestic customers for speculative purposes and also intensified their lending activities outside Japan. This left them heavily exposed, first when Japan's domestic bubble burst in the early 1990s, and then again in 1997 when the Asian Economic Crisis hit. Choy (1999) argues that banks and regulators might have been able to handle any of these developments singularly, but lost control when facing them simultaneously.

With the failure of some second tier banks the crisis of the Japanese banking industry found its first victims in 1994 and 1995. Developments accelerated in pace with the failure of an important bank, Hokkaido Taishoku Bank, and a major securities house, Yamaichi Securities, in 1997. The Japanese government finally reacted with a scheme to bail out banks through the injection of public funds, and by March 1998 15 out of the 19 major Japanese banks had received government funding. In addition, two banks, the Long-Term Credit Bank and Nippon Credit Bank, were nationalized and four regional banks were put into receivership. To receive public funding banks had to commit to restructuring their operations, and measures included the commitment to reduce employment by 20,000 employees as well as the closure of 10% of branches (Choy 1999).

The need to restructure and to increase profitability also led to a merger wave between banks, reducing the number of major banks (city banks) from 13 to only 5. The crisis in Japanese banking continued, however, and while some of the larger banking groups were targeting positive results again, the Japanese government still considered it necessary to nationalize two troubled banks, the Resona Banking Group (formerly the Asahi and Daiwa Bank) in May 2003 and Ashikaga Bank in December 2003 (Miyajima and Yafeh 2003).

Based on the so-called Big Bang plan of 1996 that saw the abolition of barriers between banks, securities and insurance companies, banks also strengthened ties with other financial institutions, partly integrating operations. Thus, the developments in the banking industry took place within the larger consolidation and reorganization of Japan's financial industries (Hoshi and Kashyap 1999, Miyajima and Yafeh 2003, Choy 1999). For the period from 2001 to 2003 statistics show a reduction in the number of bank branches from 15,315 to 14,190, and of employees from 352,805 to 317,805 (Japanese Bankers Association, various years). Securities companies between the years 1995 and 2003 reduced employment from 118,811 to 85,027 people. While there was a reduction of sales personnel engaged in outside sales activities, the group mostly affected were internal administrative staff with a reduction of over 22,000 people (Nihon Shōkengyō Kyōkai, no year). Life insurance companies reduced their branch networks from a peak of 21,950 branch offices in 1992 to 15,232 in 2002. Employment of internal administrative staff was reduced during the same period from 105,000 to 75,000 people (Saito 2004).

In terms of how the development of human resources was affected, some parallels to the electronics industry exist. Like electronics companies, banks reduced their workforces. Trying to save on costs and also shifting weight towards more personnel-intensive consumer services, banks also increased the number of non-regular employees. As for the manufacturing sector, the management of the remaining regular employees became a major issue. Employers had to keep personnel costs stable or even reduce them, but at the same time needed to motivate employees to develop new skills and to take on more responsibilities. Banks tried to realize these objectives by doing away with seniority-based systems of remuneration and advancement and replacing them with merit-oriented ones. Finally, the management of female employees became an issue with the need to provide equal employment opportunities.

In reducing workforces, banks resorted to the same measures as the large electronics manufacturers: freezing the hiring of fresh graduates and at the same time asking employees to retire early. For example, in 2003 the Mizuho group planned to bring down employment from 27,900 in March 2003 to 24,000 in March 2006. The figures are similar for other banking groups: UFJ Group – 22,327 to 19,750, Mitsui Sumitomo – 24,024 to 20,900, Mitsui Trust Group – 6,021 to 4,500 (*Asahi Shinbun* 20 September 2003).

A few examples in more detail: To reduce personnel costs by 10% Shizuoka Bank reduced the number of employees by 500 to roughly 4,400. Decreasing administrative staff by 220 and further reducing headquarters staff by 90 employees the bank also planned to reduce its counter staff by 200 employees. The bank hoped to partly compensate for this reduction by raising productivity through the introduction of information technology; nevertheless its main strategy was a massive increase of non-regular employees engaged in sales and customer-related services by 350 people. Adjusting the management of its regular employees the bank removed seniority-related principles and increased the weight of merit-based wage components (*Nihon Kinyū Shinbun* 20 December 2001).

Another example of such a strategy was seen in Daishi Bank. The bank also increased the number of part-timers and now employs 1,000 part-time employees to staff its counters (*KS* 25 April 2002). While Daishi Bank's move was clearly motivated by cost reductions (part-time employees are paid significantly less than regular employees) other banks tried to reduce costs and at the same time utilize the skills some part-timers may possess. Thus Saikyo Bank decided to employ female part-timers or contract employees with previous experience in the sales of insurance or other financial products that so far had largely been handled by inexperienced young male employees (*NSS* 10 April 2003).

The increase in part-timers has led to some concerns about service quality. Thus Hyakugo Bank, aiming for a labor composition of 2,000 regular employees and 1,000 part-timers (part-timers largely in charge of customer services) introduced centralized training for part-timers with a group of trainers regularly visiting its branches (*KS* 11 March 2003). Banks also took the first steps to motivate part-timers to upgrade qualifications or even change their employment status. For example, in 2003 Tottori Bank offered 10 part-time employees the opportunity to change their status to regular employees (*NKS* 10 July 2003).

However, the most interesting aspect of the human resources management of banks is the management of regular employees. As in the electronics industry, companies came forward with a number of initiatives, many of which attempted to tackle the rigidities of seniority-based remuneration and advancement systems.

The starting point for these initiatives was a reduction in wages. Regular employees in the banking sector were assured very stable careers with regular advancement through the ranks and gradual salary increases that would eventually reach very high levels. However, after coming under closer government supervision banks had to promise to reduce labor costs. Apart from sending older workers into early retirement and increasing the number of part-time employees, companies also directly reduced salaries. Salary reductions were substantial, with one newspaper article estimating that a section head aged in his early thirties who would have earned an annual salary of 10 million yen previously would only have an annual income of 7 million yen after the changes (*NKS* 25 November 2003).

In addition, banks flattened hierarchies. Shizuoka Bank moved from a system of 11 ranks to only 4 ranks (*NKS* 22 September 2001), Kansai Bank removed the position of section manager (*kachō*) (*KS* 2 March 2001) and Hokkaido Bank began a trial to eliminate managerial positions below branch manager in its branches and below the position of department heads in its head office (*NKS* 24 May 2002). Gifu Bank made branch managers responsible for running two branches at the same time (*KS* 25 August 2002).

The flattening of hierarchies, the reduction of work forces, and the closure of branches, in addition to the merger of companies, led to a decrease in advancement opportunities. Nevertheless, capable young employees had to be retained and motivated, and companies responded to this need mainly through changes in remuneration systems and by offering more advancement opportunities to younger employees. Mitsui Sumitomo Bank abolished regular seniority-based wage increments. In addition, it reduced salaries across the board and redistributed part of this sum as merit-based rewards. The bank also reduced the tenure required for advancement to branch manager from 18 to 12 years (*NKS* 25 November 2003, 4 April 2004). The Bank of Yokohama introduced a merit-based system in which responsibility and difficulty of job scope accounted for 60% of the salary compared to 20% before the reform. It also introduced a performance-based component into its retirement allowances. Family and meal allowances were eliminated. Career paths became less complex and as a result the average age of branch managers has fallen from 45 to 43 years (*NSS* 27 May 2003, *KS* 23 July 2002). In August 2003 the *Nihon Keizai Shinbun* dedicated a short article to the fact that the Mizuho group had appointed a 36-year-old employee as branch manager (*NKS* 16 August 2003).

Finally, some companies have made changes to the management of their female employees. An important development in this regard has been the scrapping of distinctions between the managerial (*sōgō shoku*) and the clerical track (*ippan shoku*). Asahi Bank abolished the separation and ranked all employees on one scale. Employees on the former clerical track can now become branch managers and can also earn more than colleagues of the same tenure on the former managerial track (NKS 7 March 2003). These changes have again garnered the interest of the press, which reported in January 2004 that Mitsubishi Trust and Banking Corporation had appointed its first female branch manager (KS 30 January 2004). The Bank of Yokohama already had 4 female branch managers at the beginning of 2004 and planned to increase the number by 2005 to 10 (KS 26 March 2004). Lastly, Juhachi Bank appointed its first two female branch managers in 2003 (KS 9 January 2003).

2.3   Retailing

As for the electronics industry and the banking sector, the Japanese retail sector has undergone tremendous changes since the 1990s. Competition has intensified significantly. Some leading established retail companies were forced into bankruptcy while many others had to undergo serious restructuring. Surviving companies are seriously challenged by quickly expanding domestic newcomers as well as by foreign retailers that have shed their reluctance to enter the Japanese retail market. As for the banking and electronics industries, changes can be related to a number of underlying factors such as the need to cope with ill-advised investment projects of the bubble economy, changes in consumer behavior, deregulation, and internationalization (Meyer-Ohle 2003, Dawson and Larke 2004).

The first development was the easing of regulations concerning the opening of large stores. Relaxed regulations for the opening of new stores have made it easier for retailers to expand store networks. In this regard, it has often been less established companies that have taken the initiative and thereby increased the competition in Japanese retailing tremendously. Companies such as electronics discounter Yamada Denki, apparel fashion retailer Fast Retailing, or drugstore chain Matsumotokiyoshi used the 1990s to rapidly build up store networks and establish themselves firmly among the leading players in Japanese retailing. While the market was, until the early 1990s, relatively firmly divided into a large store sector with a number of leading general merchandising companies (with affiliated convenience store chains) and departmental store companies on one side, and a large number of small-scale family run enterprises on the other side, this order was overthrown during the 1990s with new companies entering the market and consumers rapidly accepting their concepts. Building their success not only on short-term-oriented discount strategies but on long-term systematic development of their business models along the whole value chain and across all functions, these companies have not only challenged the market share of established retailers but have also revealed inefficiencies in their management (Meyer-Ohle 2003).

At the same time, some of the larger general merchandising and department store companies had to undergo bankruptcy proceedings. This was partly due to the increased competition of the 1990s, but at the core of their problems were mostly ill-fated diversification decisions made during the 1980s. Overall, Japanese mass-retailing entered into a period of consolidation, a process that has not yet come to an end. Among the companies that had to apply for bankruptcy protection and restructuring were major retailers like Nagasakiya, Mycal and Sogo. Other retailers like Daiei and the Saison Group were only kept alive through massive concessions by their creditors and had to sell off large parts of their operations.

All these developments took place in a setting of stagnant consumer demand and falling prices. Due to the collapse of the bubble economy, increases in mobility, and economic uncertainties in regard to old-age and job security, consumers became more cost-conscious and selective in their shopping habits. Increased competition and depressed demand led to a drop in consumer prices (Sezon Sōgō Kenkyūjo 2000).

These developments put the management of Japanese retail corporations under immense pressure to reduce costs. Due to intensified competition this could usually not be achieved by reducing the quality of assortments and services. In fact, the opposite was true; to keep up with competitors most companies had to increase service levels, for example a number of companies extended opening hours considerably, many stores staying open long into the evening or even around the clock. Other retailers moved away from self-service by increasing the attention given to customers in their shops (*Nikkei MJ* 14 August 2003).

As for electronics manufacturers and the banking sector, the above developments had serious implications for the management of human resources. While some retailers reduced personnel and initiated changes in the management of their regular employees, the management of part-time employees has become the main concern in retailing. Retailers increased the number of part-timers in their workforces to levels of up to and even beyond 80% and in this process shifted more and more tasks and responsibilities to part-time employees.

Aiming for a higher proportion of part-time employees most companies did not resort to direct strategies such as early retirement programs to reduce the number of regular employees. Instead most companies froze the hiring of new employees for a certain period of time. For example, to decrease the number of regular employees by 20% Aeon decided in May 2002 to freeze the hiring of new employees for two years. Aiming to reduce the ratio of labor costs to sales from 12% to 9% it increased the number of part-timers at the same time (*NKS* 1 May 2002). Coop Sapporo made the news in April 2004 with the announcement that it would recruit employees on regular contracts again after abstaining from doing so for 7 years. The company had reduced the number of regular employees to only 300 while increasing the number of part-time employees to 4,600 part-time employees. The average age of regular employees had increased to 42 years (*NRSMJ* 13 January 2004).

The relatively few companies that resorted to early retirement exercises were mostly companies with acute problems such as Daiei, which conducted several early retirement exercises. Another company that introduced an early retirement program was Marui, but for a different reason. It did so in response to demands from its union to provide employees with a way to opt out of a reorganization scheme that included the transfer of 95% of Marui's employees to separate companies on radically changed remuneration and advancement packages (*KS* 10 September 2003, *NKS* 12 February 2004, *NMJ* 10 February 2004).

A company that did not want to wait for a gradual change was Seiyu, under the leadership of Wal-Mart. Striving to attain an 80%

proportion of part-time employees Seiyu openly put pressure on employees to participate in an early retirement program. Burdened with a ratio of costs of sales to sales that was around 10 percentage points higher than that of its parent company Wal-Mart, Seiyu decided to cut its number of regular employees, which was 8,000, by 40%. To encourage employees to retire early Seiyu introduced a strict classification system of employees to be used in case it could not find enough volunteers. In pursuing its objectives the company was not overly concerned with union opposition or negative effects on the morale of its employees, having established that union funding for a strike would last no longer than two days and that it could continue to operate most of its stores based on its pool of 15,000 part-time workers. Because of the way pressure was openly used and also due to the relatively low retirement allowances paid, the initiative by Seiyu and Wal-Mart was seen as having introduced a new resolve into the management of human resources in Japan (*NRSMJ* 19 February 2004, *NRSMJ* 20 January 2004, *NRSMJ* 23 April 2003).

While increasing the number of part-time employees is still widely seen mainly as a tool for reducing labor costs it must still be acknowledged that some companies have made significant changes in the way part-time employees are managed. Part-time employees have practically taken over the running of sales floors, and consequently, even more than in banking, where this trend has only just begun, retailers are concerned about how this might affect the quality of customer services (*NKS* 23 April 2004).

Initiatives to increase the number of part-timers, and changes in regard to their employment conditions expanded over the whole spectrum of retail operations. Ito Yokado, an operator of general merchandising stores, which used approximately 51,000 part-timers, opened positions in store management and procurement to part-timers. The company stated it needed fresh views concerning the running of its stores regardless of whether they came from part-timers or regular employees. Consequently, Ito Yokado began to promote part-timers to the position of assistant store manager (*NKS* 7 October 2004, *NKS* 4 April 2002).

Ito Yokado's competitor, Aeon, which employs approximately 79,000 part-timers, expressed its aim of raising the proportion of part-timers from 73% to 80%. It introduced a new qualification scheme that gave part-timers the opportunity for advancement and that did *career tracks for part time*

not distinguish between part-time and regular employees. The company wanted to employ 2,000 part-timers in leadership positions by the year 2004; eventually leading to a system that pays equal wages for equal work and offers advancement possibilities regardless of initial employment status (*NKS* 5 January 2001, *NRSMJ* 25 April 2002, *NRSMJ* 11 March 2004).

Sapporo Coop, where, as already mentioned, part-timers accounted for more than 90% of employees, abolished regular salary increments based on the length of service of part-timers and instead introduced three career development paths leading up to store manager (*NRSMJ* 4 September 2004). Tairaya, a food supermarket with a heavy localized range of fresh merchandise, promoted part-timers up to the level of section manager, arguing that it is female part-timers who know most about customers' demands (*NKS* 25 August 2001). Another supermarket operator, Izumi, introduced four different ranks for part-timers and pays part-timers in the highest rank (which includes sales floor responsibility and ordering of merchandise) bonuses that equate to up to 90% of those of regular employees (*NKS* 28 December 2002). Finally, Rogers, a general discounter, has introduced a 360-degree evaluation scheme that includes part-timers and can lead to top scorers receiving hourly wages of up to 2,000 yen compared to a previous wage range between 800 and 1,400 yen (*NRSMJ* 17 October 2002).

Japanese retailers are also changing the management of their regular employees. As in the electronics and banking sector, companies are introducing systems that emphasize merit over seniority and give younger workers a chance to advance faster. Again, companies have come up with different approaches. Max Value Tohoku, a company in the Aeon group, decided in late 2002 to employ all fresh high school graduates initially on a non-regular contract. Previously many employees had left the company without fulfilling their first contracts. To receive a regular contract, employees now have to work as contract employees for a certain period and pass a test. While they lose out on some social benefits and regular wage increases, the company emphasized that its advancement decisions were overall based on merit principles and that new employees would therefore not be disadvantaged in the medium and long term (*NRSMJ* 12 October 2002). At the end of 2003, Tokyu Department Store introduced an annual salary system based on merit. Applying the system to all of its employees regardless of tenure and position was seen as a first in the Japanese department store industry. The system might lead to salary reductions of up to 20% for some employees, and it also reduced retirement payouts by 25% across the board (*NRSMJ* 25 November 2003). Ito Yokado and Seven Eleven introduced an open recruitment system for all management positions, giving all regular employees and part-timers the opportunity to apply for advertised positions. Introducing this system, the companies wanted to expand opportunities for younger employees (*NRSMJ* 19 March 2002).

Marui made one of the boldest moves in reorganizing activities. It transferred 95% of its employees to existing or newly set up functional subsidiaries in late 2002. At subsidiaries employees found radically changed employment conditions with wages on average 15% below industry level and pay and advancement based on merit and not seniority principles. In addition, the company abolished one of the core elements of the Japanese employment system, the retirement allowance, aiming to motivate its employees to "work hard and earn high from the beginning." The *Nikkei Kinyū Shinbun* cited a Morgan Stanley analyst who welcomed the initiative of the company as the first decisive move in the retail industry to transform personnel costs from fixed into variable costs (*KS* 10 September 2003, *NRSMJ* 10 February 2004).

However, not all companies are going so far in their moves to reorganize. In 2001 the management of rapidly growing discount apparel chain Shimamura expressed its commitment to its existing wage system based on seniority and skills. Trying to identify store managers among its female part-timers the company has tried to control increases in the number of regular employees and has also decided not to hire mid-career employees (*NRSMJ* 29 February 2001).

2.4 Putting developments into perspective – raising questions

Capelli (1999), looking at changes in the employment system of the U.S. argued that four major factors had threatened organizations from the 1980s onwards and driven change in employment practices. The first change was more competitive product markets that not only led to cost pressures but also reduced time to market and thereby reduced the certainty of long-term, fixed investments in capital and labor. The second change was information technology that reduced the need for monitoring tasks and thereby the importance of middle management. Functions could increasingly be outsourced. The third development was new arrangements in the financial community that greatly increased the influence of shareholders in the decision making of companies. Finally, new management techniques such as profit centers, outside benchmarking and a focus on core competencies, increased the use of market principles within the firm.

Looking at the developments in Japanese corporations many of the above factors can certainly be observed. However, it seems that it was largely actual cost pressures, the need to reduce costs quickly, that drove change in Japanese employment practices from the 1990s onwards. Considering the deep entrenchment of the Japanese employment practices within Japanese society (Matanle 2003), as well as the interdependencies with other managerial practices, it is thus doubtful whether Capelli's mainly long-term trends, would, by themselves, have been sufficient to initiate major change in Japan.

In summary, looking at the initiatives in the area of human resources, a number of major developments can be outlined, many of which are still ongoing.

First, companies reduced capacity in Japan, and this not only applied to manufacturing but also to the financial sector and some retail companies. The shrinking of head offices and closures of branch offices, outlets or factories forced the exit of many employees, often through early retirement exercises, and other employees had to accept transfers to new workplaces. In addition, companies have reduced the number of new employees recruited.

Second, companies began to concentrate on core activities. Employees working in non-core areas found themselves the target of early retirement programs, transferred to new positions within or outside of the company, or saw their workplaces reorganized into separate units, often with employment conditions that differed from those in the core company.

Third, companies introduced measures to reduce labor costs, and here they focused on reducing the number of older workers, changing remuneration systems and also increasing the number of non-regular employees. Wages based on seniority made older employees attractive targets for early retirement programs. A study carried out by the Japan Association of Development for the Aged (JADA) that collects survey data on a regular basis from about 70 corporations listed in the first section of the Tokyo Stock Exchange shows a drastic increase in the proportion of employees aged over 45. In 1981 employees of this group only accounted for 22.5% of total employees. This figure increased to 44% by the year 1998, before it went down to 39.7% in 2003 (JADA 2004). While seniority does not apply to all employees and can also be found in many white-collar dominated workplaces outside Japan, the existence of seniority principles leaves a significant imprint on the overall wage situation in Japan by creating a large wage differential by age, not only for white-collar but also for blue-collar workers (JILPT 2004a, Chart 2.1). Firms also made changes to remuneration systems by cutting bonuses and benefits. Changes in remuneration systems from being seniority-based to merit-based also often included the objective of reducing overall labor costs. Chart 2.2 shows that companies made some progress in the 1990s in this regard but that wage differentials between young and older workers remained large.

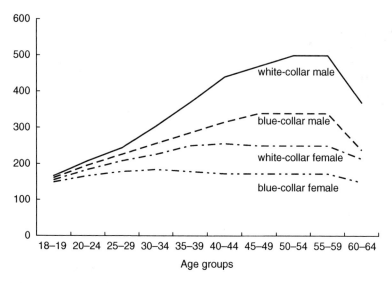

Chart 2.1 Wage profiles in manufacturing by age, sex, and occupation 2002 (monthly wage in 1000 yen)

Source: JILPT 2004a, p. 38.

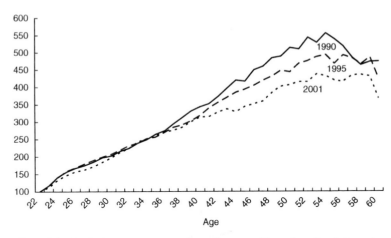

Chart 2.2   Seniority wage curve of employees with university degrees by year (monthly wage in 1000 yen)

Note: Monthly salary of new male graduates 1990: 169,900 Yen, 1995: 194,200 Yen, 2001: 198,300 Yen.

Source: based on Kōsei Rōdōshō 2003, p. 150.

Fourth, companies sought to increase flexibility and to reduce fixed costs. The main strategy here was to increase the number of non-regular workers to counter fluctuations in demand and the extension of operating hours. Companies also increased their long-term flexibility by reducing seniority-based components in remuneration. Based on cost-saving objectives and strategies to increase flexibility, the proportion of non-regular employees among the total employees increased significantly, reaching over 30% in 2004 (Table 2.1). In manufacturing, this strategy has been used by companies to reduce costs to a level that allows them to keep production activities in Japan, which is important due to the close linkages with research and development. In retailing and banking, part-time employees have largely taken over customer-oriented services, supposedly a core function for these sectors. Non-regular employees have thus attained an importance that goes far beyond acting as buffers in times of recession. For the Japanese retail sector Ribault (1999) argues that companies are striving for a new model of hyperflexibility of human resources that is heavily dependent on the use of part-timers.

Fifth, companies began to seek ways to retain and motivate capable regular employees. They had to do so in a situation where

Table 2.1 Japanese employees by type of employment (million and %)

	1987		1992		1997		2002		2004		2007	
	m	%	m	%	m	%	m	%	m	%	m	%
Total	42.1	100	48.6	100	49.4	100	49.4	100	49.4	100	51.7	100
Regular Employees	34.6	80.3	38.1	78.4	33.4	75.2	34.9	70.6	33.4	67.6	34.4	66.5
Part-time and *arubaito**	6.6	15.2	8.5	17.5	10.8	20.1	10.5	21.3	10.8	21.9	11.6	22.5
Dispatch/contract/other	1.9	4.5	2.1	4.3	4.6	4.5	4.0	8.1	4.6	9.3	5.7	11.0

Note: Labor Force Survey, estimate based on monthly survey of 40,000 households with roughly 100,000 people above 15 years of age (people in dependent employment, except executives and people employed in agriculture). The definition of non-regular employee categories changed from 2002 onwards. Employment categories based on terminology used by companies.
* *arubaito:* Normally used by companies for employing students and pupils while part-timer is used for partially employed women. For more detailed definitions see Chapter 5.

Source: Sōmuchō Tōkeikyoku (2005).

overall costs could not be increased and advancement opportunities were reduced through the trimming of hierarchies and work forces. Companies realized that increasing merit-based components in remuneration was one solution here and also began to put less emphasis on age and tenure when deciding on advancement.

Sixth, some companies recognized that they needed to retain and motivate capable non-regular employees since many core functions are now performed by this group of employees. To do so some companies began to differentiate and to systematize the management of non-regular employees.

The above initiatives by Japanese companies in the management of their human resources raise a number of questions concerning their importance and impact in the long run. This is especially so since experiences from the past have shown that while Japanese companies have regularly initiated changes, many of these changes were not really followed through eventually. For example, many companies at the beginning of the 1980s came up with initiatives to reduce the growth dependency of their human resources management strategies but did not follow up after the onset of the bubble economy when beliefs in the possibility of prolonged growth were revived.

Still, for several reasons the changes that were initiated from the 1990s onwards appear to have had deep and lasting consequences. Here, the disruptive nature of many of the current changes has to be discussed first. Lincoln and Nakata (1997), looking at the first stage of corporate restructuring in the early 1990s, argued that future adjustments to the Japanese employment system would probably be of an incremental and non-disruptive nature. Further, Usui and Colignon (1996) argued that Japanese companies in restructuring usually go through a certain succession of measures, but usually return to their original configuration once a cycle is completed.

Yet, pressures on Japanese corporations went beyond just recessionary pressures and therefore many corporations, some of which were leading players in their industries, gave up their reluctance towards disruptive change and began to actively challenge previous boundaries and taboos. Examples include Sanyo in the electronics industry, which did away with standardized wages for fresh graduates; Marui, which did away with retirement allowances; Max Value Tohoku, which employed fresh graduates initially as non-regular employees, and Seiyu, which introduced an early retirement system that was very close to selective dismissals in the way it was executed.

Major factors that support the durability of the current changes are their visibility as well as their symbolic importance for overall change in the Japanese economy. While labor costs do not always constitute the most critical cost component, they are substantial in the banking and the retail sectors. However, changes in human resources management are highly visible and symbolic and, as Lincoln and Nakata (1997) have argued, seem to be increasingly linked to managements wanting to demonstrate their resolve to align themselves with the interests of investors. Companies have become increasingly concerned about investor relationships, especially since many companies have a high proportion of foreign ownership. Total ownership by foreign investors reached a record high of 23.7% of total value of shares in 2005 (*NKS-NNI* 17 June 2005). Foreign ownership has reached more than 20% for each of Japan's four large banking groups, and foreign investors have a 30% stake in each of Japan's five leading pharmaceutical companies. In the past, a large number of shares were held by friendly investors who were mostly interested in the long-term development of companies or the stabilization of business relationships. For example, banks expected to be commissioned to provide banking services in exchange for holding shares in client companies. In addition, cross-shareholding arrangements were widely seen as an effective way to prevent takeovers. However, foreign investors, mainly pension and mutual funds, are seeking capital gains and dividend payouts from their investments, and Japanese companies eager for funding have promised to raise dividend payouts to international standards (Table 2.2, *NKS-/NNI* 4 June 2004a, 5 June 2004).

Apart from foreign investors increasing their stakes in Japanese companies, the management of Japanese companies was also confronted with initiatives by foreign companies in Japan. Companies under direct foreign control such as Nissan, Shinsei Bank and Seiyu all introduced reforms in human resources management early on and Japanese companies used these as examples and reference points when changing their own policies. For example, the drive of Japanese retailers to bring down personnel costs and to increase the number

Table 2.2   Examples of foreign ownership of Japanese companies

Company	Foreign ownership %
Hoya	50.7
Orix	50.5
Yamada Denki	50.1
Yamanouchi Pharmaceutical	41.0
Don Quijote	41.0
Nomura Holding	40.2
Takeda Chemical	38.0
Hitachi	31.3
UFJ Holdings	31.0
NEC	29.7
Mitsubishi Tokyo Financial Group	28.0

Sources: NKS/NNI 4 June 2004a, 5 June 2004, 4 June 2004b, 7 May 2004, 6 January 2004, 7 May 2004.

of part-timers was related to the imminent entry of Wal-Mart into the Japanese market. In the year 2000, the Long-Term Credit Bank of Japan, which was renamed Shinsei Bank after coming under foreign ownership, became a forerunner in introducing merit principles and doing away with seniority elements in remuneration (*NKS* 9 November 2002).

The questions that need to be asked now concern the role of employees in the processes of change and the consequences of the current changes for employees in their workplaces. One diary writer reminds us:

> *2 September 2003 – Of course switching jobs, starting a new business, becoming independent, dispatch work, all these can become wonderful ways to work and to live. I think it is great that such choices are increasing. However, long-term employment as a regular employee is also really one of those wonderful choices and if one has the real wish to work, one should be able to work. The Nikkei (newspaper) glorifies changing jobs or setting up a business by bringing up only success stories, and criticizes regular employees being employed long-term by bringing up non-representative cases of failure.*[3]

Thus, looking at perceptions and reactions of employees, the following points need to be discussed.

The first point concerns the restructuring activities that saw many companies reduce their personnel. Studies on the so-called downsizing activities of American companies have shown significant consequences, not only for employees who lose their jobs but also for those who stay behind. While some employees might see such measures as a way to increase the competitiveness of their company others might be worried that downsizing might become a recurring event and will eventually threaten their own livelihood. Employees might also have worries about the potential loss of capable colleagues, an increase in their workload, and loss of personal relationships.

The second point concerns changes in working conditions and principles of employment. Here it matters whether employees see those measures as ways of strengthening the role of management, as measures to cut costs, or as measures to motivate employees. This perception is important since it determines whether or not measures are seen as legitimate and just. Here Thelen and Kume (1999: 493) have argued concerning wage systems that *"abolishing seniority wages appears to be less of a neoliberal strategy against labor than it is a mechanism for achieving advantage against other firms in competition for the best new recruits."* Indeed, many companies are introducing remuneration and promotion systems that increase opportunities for younger employees and many companies have actively drawn the public's attention to cases where they have promoted young employees early into positions of responsibility. Still, it must be asked how employees themselves have seen these measures and whether they have understood the companies' intentions. The fact that companies did not want to increase overall labor costs and thus might have to redistribute resources from older to younger workers might still lead to legitimacy concerns. Therefore, ambiguities among employees concerning the changing principles of employment can be expected and it can be asked whether differences in opinions are found only along generational lines.

The next point is the significant change in the composition of workforces. Companies have increased the number of non-regular workers such as part-timers, contractual employees, dispatch-workers, or workers being employed with subcontractors. While Japanese companies have always employed a certain number of non-regular employees, they have often been utilized rather randomly. The initiatives outlined above show a significant sophistication in the use of non-regular employees. Companies have been shifting whole functions that were formerly performed by regular employees alone or together with part-timers to non-regular employees only. However, it must be asked whether companies can sustain a significant gap between core and non-core employees with differences in career opportunities in the long run (Thelen and Kume 1999). Especially in the retail sector, which has already accumulated experience in the utilization and management of part-timers, some companies seem to have already realized this problem and have come up with ways to manage non-regular employees more systematically by differentiating remuneration and offering part-time employees the opportunity to advance within the company. However, again it must be asked whether such measures are seen as sufficient by non-regular employees.

The change in the composition of workforces potentially has major consequences not only for people in non-regular employment but also for regular employees. It has been argued that non-regular employment used to be basically structured according to the needs of people who could not take up full-time employment due to other obligations. However, it is increasingly the needs of companies in regard to cost-reductions and flexibility that determines the demand for and modes of non-regular work, and it needs to be asked how employees react to these demands. The important questions are why and with what expectations do non-regular employees take up such work and how do they view the differences between their own treatment and that of regular employees. For regular employees it needs to be asked how they view non-regular employees and how the addition of more non-regular employees affects their workplaces.

The overall question is therefore how employees regard the changes in the employment system. Capelli observed that in the US workers have faced the new realities by increasing their marketability, and once markets turned in their favor then sought their own advantages by changing jobs more frequently or by demanding higher wages (Capelli 1999). Looking at the restructuring measures introduced by Japanese companies in the 1990s Dirks argued that *"so far, Japanese firms have been able to restructure and adjust to difficult environments without endangering the basic social contract with*

their workforce, according the latter a considerably strong sense of employ-
ment security" (Dirks 1999: 269). While Japanese companies have
pressured some employees into early retirement they generally seem
determined to continue to offer their employees long-term employment security (Matanle 2003). However, the question that will have
to be answered is whether employees will be satisfied with the new
deal offered by employers in which a certain degree of long-term
employment security is paired with high possible individual rewards
but also with greatly increased uncertainty concerning remuneration and advancement.

Another question to keep in mind is whether Japan will again see
the development of relatively uniform employment practices among
large corporations or whether corporations will consciously use differences in employment practices as a means to differentiate themselves from competitors? Surveys among employees show a widening
range of values in regard to employment, and by changing and differentiating their practices companies might in fact come closer to
meeting the needs of a more diverse workforce.

This chapter has looked at Japanese management from a micro-
perspective by providing examples of single companies, especially
large companies. The results may well reflect what Capelli (1999:
113) expressed regarding the situation in the US, with some developments not yet showing their significance when viewed in general
terms but being very significant when viewed from the viewpoint of
the single worker and company. For Japan, it has been argued that it
is exactly the employment patterns in large corporations that have
provided social stability as well as ideals to be strived for, not only by
those in school and universities and their families but also by smaller
companies in the treatment of their own employees (Matanle 2003).
With patterns in large corporations clearly changing it will be interesting to see what new ideals will develop.

Finally, it can be asked how far changes will go and how the different developments are interrelated. Regarding the US, Capelli
(1999) sees a general shift in the way workers and their motivational
patterns are viewed by management, and argues that the "happy
worker" model was replaced by a "frightened worker" model during
the 1980s.

Admittedly this would be quite a dramatic development for
Japan, and within the corporate initiatives outlined above such

inclinations have not appeared. Still, there might be some employees who perceive the situation in this way. In the following, employee perspectives will thus be discussed in more detail, beginning with views on restructuring, followed by perceptions on changing principles of work, and finally by perspectives on non-regular employment.

3
Experiencing Corporate Reorganization

5 October 1998 – Bright and clear weather

The other day, Nissan, which entered into collaboration with Renault, announced a large-scale restructuring exercise. I think that according to this policy 20 to 30,000 employees will be restructured, out of a total of 140,000 employees, including those at affiliated companies. It seems that even this has not been viewed positively overseas (even more employees should have become the target of rationalization), but within Japan this plan is already considered to be quite harsh.

Inside our company we talk about Nissan being in a serious situation as if we were not involved ourselves, but somehow it appears that our company's situation has also worsened. In the future, areas of business that were once cultivated as pillars of business to compare favorably with our core business will fail entirely, and pressure is mounting to scale down operations. In addition, research facilities that have been supporting new fields of business will become useless and there seem to be plans for reorganization.

The department where I am working is no exception; it looks as if a big purge will be carried out at the year end; a plan for large scale reshuffling and transfers to other companies. According to rumors, revitalization will be to the extent of dispatching employees for support to assembly plants of car companies (Being inserted into the assembly-line system, the manufacturing of car parts is very, very tough, dreary work beyond imagination).[4]

The above diary entry was written under the somewhat paradoxical headline "bright and clear weather" (the writer reports daily on the weather). The writer understands the situation of his company very well, and while he does not fear for his own job, he still expresses concern that his work situation might change radically after being sent to another company.

While the above writer talks about transfers to other companies, a more radical measure to reduce employee numbers was the so-called voluntary early retirement exercise.

> *29 August 2001 – It seems that the second restructuring of the year will happen and that until Friday this week the company will recruit voluntary early retirees. Of course, I don't feel like retiring. But, maybe half of the people we currently employ will have to. If this is so, things might become awful. If there are no volunteers, it will lead to dismissals. I am worried about whether I can stay.*[5]

The writer of this entry expresses his own anxieties, yet only hints at the complexities involved in retirement programs, a point that is further developed by the next writer, who addresses issues such as pressures being exerted, people leaving unexpectedly, and his own sadness at seeing the departure of colleagues who had supported him previously.

> *30 October 2001 – As I have written previously, the applications for this program (just call it restructuring) had to come in by yesterday, and altogether 62 people applied. Because the targeted number of 60 was reached, the drive for participants has come to an end. It is said that in this process various patterns of human behavior have unfolded. There were people who have persistently received demands and suggestions from superiors to retire early, other people retired really unexpectedly – various things seem to have happened. While many people will retire by the end of November, most people will leave earlier through paid vacations, flex time and other measures. From my workplace two people will be on vacation from around the tenth. I have just been a great nuisance to those two people and I am indebted to them in a way that I cannot find words to express. I am feeling extremely sad.*[6]

The above diary entries address two of the main methods that Japanese companies have used in their drive to reduce employment numbers: inter-company transfers and early retirement exercises. Those measures stand out as they not only involve a radical change in working conditions, but because they break up existing relationships among employees through the movement of a large number of people.

A survey of 1,038 male panel members, conducted over two days in November 2001 by Internet survey company Macromill (2003), reported on restructuring activities as seen by employees. Most employees either reported that so-called restructuring was carried out in their companies (12.1%), is currently being conducted (31.8%) or will probably be conducted (29.9%). Concerning the measures carried out, most employees mentioned voluntary early retirement exercises (50.2%), followed by large cuts in salaries and bonuses (31.8%), internal redeployment (28.3%), temporary transfers between companies (25.5%), permanent transfers between companies (21.9%), forced retirements (19.5%), dismissals (12.7%) and finally demotions (10.3%). The size of companies largely determined the methods adopted by companies. Employees of small companies with less than 100 employees reported dismissals (30.9%) and cuts in salary and bonuses (44.4%) while employees of larger companies with more than 1,000 employees reported early retirement programs (62.4%) and transfers between companies (35.1%) (Macromill 2003).

This chapter will thus take a deeper look into the issue of restructuring by considering two measures: transfers and early retirement exercises.

3.1 Being transferred to another company: chance or dead end street?

The possibility of transferring employees between companies has been described as one of the most interesting features of the Japanese employment system (Dirks 1999). By transferring employees, companies can circumvent some of the rigidities of a system where the relationship between employers and employees is based on the assumption of long-term employment. In exchange for employment security employees are expected to readily comply with demands for transfers between different functions of the company, between different locations in and outside Japan, and finally even to other companies. These may be affiliates or subsidiaries of the company workers are employed at but can also be other companies such as suppliers, customers or financial institutions.

There are two types of transfers between companies. The first type, called *shukkō*, sees companies delegate employees to another company with the original employment contract remaining intact, thereby assuring the employee continuity in terms of income, working conditions, and job stability. The second type of transfer, *tenseki*, sees the original employment contract become invalid and employees becoming permanent employees of the company they are transferred to. As will be seen from the diary entries, transfers often happen in a sequence. Employees are first delegated to another company under a *shukkō* agreement before their status is changed to *tenseki*.

Since transfers are significant events, people frequently bring them up in their blogs. Issues addressed include perceptions about people who have been transferred, the way a transfer was decided on and conducted, differences in working conditions between former and new workplaces, and consequences for work places after colleagues were transferred.

The narrative on experience that people have with transfers begins with a blog writer's account of the complexities that people face within the restructuring of Japanese corporations. The author of the diary entry writes about colleagues being called back to what is described as the former parent company.

26 December 2002 – Extremely sad shouts by middle-aged men ... Scary restructuring is carried out. Today there seems to be restructuring at the company where I am working. People who are to be restructured are not allowed to go out today ... It is just that restructuring does not mean being axed but being called back to the former parent company. However, the employment conditions seem to worsen drastically. This is how things have become. Pitiful ... In the end, 30 regular employees fell to restructuring by being sent on so-called temporary transfer to the former parent. Most of them are in their forties. Yet, everyone I normally talk to or get along well with has been restructured. Two of them are even in their thirties ... All things considered, the cut in people was overdone. In my section, everyone above section chief is gone. How will work be distributed? What will become of things like settling the accounts? Somehow, even being left behind may become hell.[7]

The writer points out that most of the employees transferred back to the former parent company were in their forties and some of them were even in senior positions. The fact that they were sent back and forth shows the long-lasting and complex responsibilities that Japanese companies assume for their employees. The extract also shows the anxieties of someone who is left behind.

Other diary entries also highlight that downsizing measures mostly target older employees, such as the following report of a diary writer on her husband's class reunion.

14 April 2002 – Yesterday night was the first class reunion in five years. So far at class reunions usually about 30 people have come together. But, yesterday night it was only 15 people, including the teachers who had taught the class...Again and again, those who attended last night talked about gloomy topics such as salarymen being loaned out to subsidiaries, self-employed people whose business is in a slump, etc. etc. My husband's generation has been described as "company men" or "men who exist to work," but most of the people are only working like mad because of the intense competition. Indeed, there are some people who have attained positions of some sort by doing so. However, they are also of the generation that is most likely to be subjected to restructuring. There were many people who were directly affected by the recent prolonged recession. In last night's conversations, the thought was resignedly brought up that "Tonight, we who are able to attend may be the ones who are still doing ok."[8]

As explained, there are two types of transfers between companies, temporary and permanent ones, with the two often happening in sequence. The change from one to the other usually goes along with a change in conditions, with salaries being adjusted to the level of the company that employees are delegated to – in the case of the writer below this meant a wage cut of between 20 and 30%.

25 May 2001 – The company's "Reform and Renewal Plan" has become quite clear with the publication of the branch committee's report. The status of employees who are currently on temporary transfer will be changed to permanent transfer after paying them a retirement allowance. Of course there will be a salary cut of 20 to 30%. This will be carried out in March next year. The restructuring will bring much pain. After this, I don't know what will happen in my own workplace.[9]

However, employees have to agree to a change in status, and it seems that this is not always achieved without pressure. The following writer describes the case of a friend who refused such a change of status and afterwards found himself stripped of most of his responsibilities, separated into a different corporate unit, and told to find a new workplace.

> *4 October 2002 – Is the company bad? Or the people? – This afternoon there was a phone call from a friend who has been loaned out to an associated company. He asked me to tell him about the recent changes concerning the retirement system. In his company, all employees on temporary transfer above 50 years of age have been pressed to accept permanent transfers. Including him, there are very few who have firmly refused; all the others have chosen to retire or to accept the change in status ...*
>
> *Both of us were of the same rank but lately his subordinates have been assigned to another manager and it seems that he was transferred to a provisional organizational unit along with others who have refused the change in status ... I asked him about the actual situation in his company and was surprised. It seems that lately, every other day he has been told in private interviews to find work for himself, by himself, or to retire if he can't find it. It seems that management gathered up employees who are to be cut and said grandly: "As we can't find a new workplace for all of you, please look for work by yourself." Since it is a temporary unit and there is no intention of thinking seriously about a shared future, I felt this was similar to the relationship between a warden and a prisoner.*[10]

Notably, in an earlier entry the same author talks about the problems he encountered when having to force an employee to retire from the company. The possibility of transfers provided superiors with a way to ease the effects of restructuring on their subordinates, but at the same time created a responsibility for superiors to find suitable positions.

> *27 June 2002 – I was reluctant but I made employees retire. According to the company's instruction that only high-performing employees are needed, etc. I took part in a cost reduction program that forced out older*

people (equals high salary) and so one of my staff members, who is 55, had to retire. There was no reason that would justify firing him; until now he has completed his duties, it was just that it was necessary to reduce the number of employees by one, so he was made redundant from July onwards. Had this happened in the past, there would have been a position for him somewhere for the five years he had left until retirement, but nowadays redundant employees just become targets for elimination.

For nearly two months, he and I both searched around for another work-place for him, but subsidiaries are also reducing the number of older employees and one can only move if one has many personal connections, so he was finally driven into accepting retirement. Unexpectedly, this Tuesday we found a subsidiary to which it seemed he could transfer on a permanent basis. This was soon negotiated and yesterday (Wednesday) he had an interview with the president of that company. A permanent transfer was promptly decided; in other words, it was decided that he will retire from the parent company and be re-employed at the subsidiary. Today the retirement paperwork was concluded and tomorrow is his farewell party. At first glance, this seems to be a happy ending but why it is not possible for him to be loaned out; in other words, keeping his status as a parent company employee and continue working at the subsidiary without retiring? Since I have no authority there is nothing that can be done. Still I am angry at the company's pitiless system.[11]

The next excerpt shows the desperation of an employee who after being delegated to another company faces problems in the tasks he has to perform.

20 April 2000 – From today I will be loaned out and thrown into another company....Not only that, my commuting time has increased by 30 minutes and it seems that I need to put together software I don't really understand and VC++ [visual C] is (extremely) difficult. What to do? (T_T) I thought that I would understand it if I looked at it a little but I don't understand it at all...What should I do? I have cried already. Perhaps I should make my junior do it and escape (explode). On top of this I have to do the software support for our company. Isn't that inconsiderate? I don't know.[12]

Complex issues also arise due to employees being affiliated with two different organizations. The author of the diary entry below was promoted but is unsure of the reasons. Was he promoted because of his performance or his seniority? Who has evaluated him? The implementation of result-oriented remuneration and advancement systems will be further outlined in a following chapter, but it seems to add an additional layer of difficulty to the already complicated issue of personnel transfers between companies.

> *18 November 2002 – Granted a promotion for the first time in my life. From ordinary employee to assistant manager. Normally, one should be happy. But, I'm a loaned out employee and my salary comes from the place I was loaned to, and I am already getting a higher salary than at my original workplace (though this is strange too). So the senior staff allowance, 1,500 yen (cheap!!), is not reflected in the present salary. It really is just an appointment on paper. Moreover, who is judging me, as a loaned employee? The advancement of a loaned out employee is slower than that of one who is not loaned out. Also, under the same appointment order, I will be promoted to assistant manager together with someone who is a junior by one year who is also a subsection chief. What is this? Am I considered leftovers? (Laughs) Therefore, although they have said that performance-oriented measures have been introduced, in the end it is still the seniority system. When promoting my junior, I feel that they thought "Ah, we forgot about Endo." That's why I'm not very happy.[13]*

Another writer who is himself an employee delegated by his original company describes himself as not having to worry in a situation where many of his colleagues might lose their jobs.

> *23 August 2004 – As I am an employee who has been loaned out by the parent company to the present company, the company's dissolution has no direct consequences for me. In order to settle the company's debts, once the company is dissolved, the regular employees will be dismissed. Hiring interviews for the new company will begin immediately. With this commotion there will be a surprise. No one can concentrate on his work.[14]*

Finally, having to work with employees whose primary employment contract is not with the company, co-workers raise questions about the sincerity of such employees in fulfilling their tasks.

21 February 2004 – Today it's a complaint about a superior which I have been thinking about writing for some time. Due to him, I became infected with the wish to quit soon after joining the company. Well, it may be that one rarely comes across a good superior, but still. This problematic man will soon be 60. He worked in some company's sales division before. His position is head. Now he is working here while being loaned out from another company. This is the second workplace prepared for this lucky guy since his retirement. In spite of being in such a lucky position, how can it be that he has no spirit at all? Being the head of the sales office you would think that he would be out all the time, but he does not move at all and always sticks to the office ... As things are, there are many who want to work but cannot work ... even if they try their best, there are people who get pay cuts or are restructured ... Especially in my case, I have experienced my company going bankrupt and losing my job! People who have no intention to work should retire properly! (Sorry ... I was too emotional)[15]

The perceptions of employees concerning transfers as shown above need some further categorization and qualification. Obviously transfers happen in different situations and for different purposes. Suzuki (1996) categorizes the following four types of temporary transfers.

- Transfers because of shortages of personnel with necessary skills: employees are delegated that possess skills that receiving companies need. Often these are companies smaller than the delegating firm, or businesses that are undergoing reorganization.
- Training type: employees are delegated to gain experience they cannot gain in their original businesses.
- Exchange type: employees are delegated to mix with employees from other companies.
- Personnel reduction: employees are delegated because companies have no adequate positions for them, especially middle-aged managers for whom the corporate hierarchy is too narrow to advance. Here also, age linked salaries play a role, with companies being able to reduce their own wage bill.

Suzuki (1996) states that two types of temporary transfers have gained special importance during the 1990s. The first is downsizing related transfers where not only older employees but increasingly also younger employees are affected. These transfers are often just a stepping stone towards permanent transfers and companies often exploit the significantly different working conditions between larger and smaller companies; smaller companies paying lower wages and offering fewer benefits compared to the larger delegating company. Suzuki labels this form of transfer as a "harsh transfer." The other form of transfer that Suzuki sees as having gained popularity is the delegation of capable young employees into affiliated companies at an early stage in their career to provide them with leadership experience. This sort of experience is difficult to gain within the rigid organizational structure of larger companies where employees must first gain seniority before it is their turn to take over responsibility.

The importance of inter-company transfers of employees in the restructuring of Japanese corporations has caught the attention of researchers and public policy makers and this has led to the collection of empirical data through large scale company surveys. A survey carried out by the Japanese Ministry of Health, Labor and Welfare (on companies with more than 30 employees; response rate 90.1%, 5,326 companies) found that 37.2% of companies had transferred employees during the year 2001. The use of this practice clearly increased with company size. Only 27.1% of smaller companies with less than 99 employees use transferred workers, in contrast to a much higher figure of 92.5% for companies with more than 1,000 employees (Kōsei Rōdō Daijin Kanbō Tōkei Jōhōbu 2001). Higher numbers of employees obviously lead to more opportunities and a greater necessity to transfer workers. Transfers are often initiated by the sending side and here larger companies have a better chance of finding placements for their employees since they usually have a larger network of affiliated companies, and more leverage over customers, suppliers or other affiliated smaller companies. In addition, larger companies are more dedicated to the principles and responsibilities of lifelong employment, thereby putting greater accountability on them than on smaller companies where employees have lesser expectations of their employers.

The most detailed study on the practice of inter-company job transfers was carried out by the Japanese Institute of Labor Policy and Training (then just the Japanese Institute of Labor) in 1998 (JIL 1999) by surveying companies that delegated or received employees as well as employees who had undergone transfers. The study was biased in the sense that it purposely surveyed companies that were part of larger company groupings. Nevertheless, its results can be used to further substantiate the importance of transfers as well as their objectives and results.

The study again found that the number of employees delegated increased with company size. The 18 very large companies surveyed with more than 20,000 employees had at the time of the survey an impressive average of 5,325 people as employees who were not working for them but were delegated temporarily to other companies (*shukkō*). Employees were sent to a large number of companies, averaging (for very large companies) an equally impressive 436 companies. In addition, companies reported that an average of 296 employees had accepted a permanent transfer (*tenseki*) to another company during the year surveyed (Table 3.1).

The study also found that for the majority of companies the importance of transferring employees had increased over the previous 10 years, with 61.2% of companies seeing an increase, 30.3% no change, and only 8.4% a decrease in the number of employees transferred (JIL 1999: 8). Altogether, transferred employees accounted for 10.1% of the total workforce of companies participating in the survey, with the figure increasing from 5.1% for companies with less than 1,000 employees to 16.5% for companies with 20,000 employees and more.

Blog writers were right in their perception that the older an employee gets the higher the chances are that he will be sent to another company. On average, 22.3% of employees above 55 years of age were on transfer arrangements. This figure reached an astonishing 40.5% for companies with 10,000 to 19,999 employees and 32.4% for companies with more than 20,000 employees (JIL 1999: 9).

Companies not only delegated but also received employees, and looking at receiving companies the survey found that companies on average received employees from 1.5 other companies, with the number of persons received increasing with the size of the companies (Table 3.2).

A major issue in the discussion of transfers is whether they are initiated by the receiving or the sending side. This answer to this

Table 3.1 Number of receiving companies and number of employees delegated by size of transferring company

Company size – sending company	Receiving companies		Employees on temporary transfer		Employees permanently transferred in 1997	
	Sample size – sending companies	Average no. of receiving companies	Sample size – sending companies	Average no. of employees involved	Sample size – sending companies	Average no. of employees involved
Total (employees)	184	92.6	176	1006.5	174	49.6
Below 999	33	10.7	32	39.4	32	3.9
1000 to 4999	88	39.1	82	250.4	82	11.6
5000 to 9999	28	100.1	28	753.8	28	14.1
10000 to 19999	17	152.5	16	2,399.6	16	150.0
20000 and above	18	435.8	18	5,324.7	16	296.3

Note: Survey of 1000 large companies with many affiliates and listed on first section of the Tokyo Stock Exchange, response rate 18.8%.

Source: JIL 1999: 7.

Table 3.2 Employees received by type and size of receiving companies

Company size – receiving company	People temporarily received		People permanently received	
	Number of receiving companies	Average no. of employees involved	Number of receiving companies	Average no. of employees involved
Total (employees)	960	37.9	756	14.2
Below 99	29	15.5	21	3.5
100 to 299	562	20.4	429	8.2
300 to 999	310	46.7	252	15.9
Above 1000	59	169.9	54	57.5

Note: Survey of 5,000 companies affiliated with large companies, response rate 24.7%.
Source: JIL 1999: 10.

Table 3.3 Who initiates the transfer of employees? (answers in %)

Type/Age	% transfers based on needs of receiving company	% transfers based on demands of sending company	Does not apply
Temporary			
Below 39	52.7	21.0	26.3
40 to 49	56.3	28.0	15.3
50 to 54	44.5	42.6	12.9
Above 55	35.6	48.0	16.2
Permanent	32.1	41.1	26.8

Source: JIL 1999: 15.

question not only affects the perceptions of transferred employees themselves but also those of employees of receiving companies. Here the survey again found age to be the determining factor. While for younger employees it was normally the needs of the receiving company that led to transfers, for older employees above 50 it was often demands from the sending company that resulted in transfers. Overall, a substantial number of transfers seem to be based on demands from the sending side (Table 3.3).

taking in new employees is not easy.

Taking in employees is not unproblematic for receiving companies. While 25.6% of companies responded that transfers caused no problems, others complained about increased labor costs (50%), not getting the right people (33.2%), or employment and advancement opportunities being taken away (33.1%). Less frequently mentioned complaints included companies having reached their limits in regard to the number of transferees they felt they could take (20%), the evaluation of employees becoming difficult (15.5%) and a loss of individuality in management (15.5%) (JIL 1999). As the blog entries showed, employees seem to be well aware of these issues and this knowledge does lead to anxieties, with employees feeling that they might not be welcome in their new workplaces.

The survey also found that the average length of transfers was 3.87 years (standard deviation 2.04 years) with the average length of the most extreme cases being 13.43 years (standard deviation 8.45 years). Nevertheless, transfers often did not require the consent of the employee him/herself, although employers might still seek it. For employees from the management ranks, 61.3% of companies responded that the consent of the employee was not necessary, while for normal employees this number dropped to 47.3%. Employees of very large companies with more than 20,000 employees had to show a higher level of flexibility, with 78.9% of such companies regarding the consent of managerial employees as not being a condition for transfer, while for regular employees this figure stood at 68.4%. Permanent transfers seem by definition to require the consent of the employee since at this time the contract with the employee is terminated. Still, 10.3% of companies claimed that consent was not necessary for normal employees (for managerial employees it was 16.3%) and especially smaller companies with fewer than 1,000 employees claimed more liberties in this regard (37.9% for managerial, 25.9% for non-managerial staff) (JIL 1999: 26).

The study by the Japanese Institute of Labor also looked at perceptions of employees concerning transfers, although results seem to be biased in the sense that the sample was put together from a database of the Japan Association of Development for the Aged, which is a government-affiliated organization set up with the purpose of creating employment opportunities for elderly employees. Thus it is not surprising that the majority of respondents (58% of 1,832 respondents) were already 61 years old and older. Still, the survey provides some interesting results. Asked about problems encountered in their new companies after a transfer, 38.4% responded that nothing special came to their mind. However, 43.4% responded that the organizational atmosphere and the personal relationships differed from their previous organization. Other problematic points included a lack of cooperation by employees of the receiving company (31.1%), differences in formal and informal decision making (19.0%), too broad a field of responsibility (17.7%), operational differences even though knowledge and technologies were the same (14.2%), and finally, too narrow a scope of responsibility (8.5%) (JIL 1999: 144).

In a theoretical review, Dirks (1999) assessed inter-company transfers on three levels. On the individual level he lauded transfers as an alternative to the even more undesirable measure of lay-offs, and therefore, overall, regarded the existence of transfers as a positive motivational factor for employees. Another positive effect attributed to transfers was the assuredness of income and pension plans. Interestingly, Dirks argued that while transfers might at first put employees in a difficult new environment, challenges concerning personal relationships and tasks might still let them grow and develop eventually.

Looking at organizational development Dirks saw transfers as a transaction cost-efficient way of conveying technical and managerial expertise across companies. Companies do not just have to rely on formalized channels of information but become able to communicate informally. For receiving firms he saw lower costs in regard to the searching and hiring of personnel. He also pointed to the possibility of a continuous revitalization of organizations through the flow of personnel.

Finally, he argued that there were positive aspects concerning structural change on a macro-economic level. Since Japan does not possess properly developed external labor markets, for many smaller firms transfers are the only way to lay hands on the qualified people they need to develop their business further.

Yet, based on the perceptions and experiences of employees as outlined above and supported by the survey results, it seems to be questionable whether the above positive effects can still be achieved. While some employees indeed stressed the rewarding nature of transfers, the diaries show that in the overall debate about restructuring the punitive aspect seemed to overshadow the perceptions of employees. Indeed, faced with the need to reduce capacity, companies in Japan might have used this instrument too frequently and for too many purposes. Some employees have found themselves in a never-ending process of being shifted back and forth between companies, while for others it was just a step on the road to permanent transfers with radically changed working conditions, or finally even to early retirement.

While the above surveys, diary entries and also academic studies, e.g. Dirks (1999) or Kato (2001), have shown the importance of transfers in the restructuring activities of Japanese corporations during the 1990s, Genda (2002) argued that transfers have declined in importance and will decline further in the future, with ties between companies weakening and with larger companies losing control over smaller companies. In addition, companies have moved functions overseas and are increasingly working with international suppliers and customers, thereby weakening existing local company relationships.

Genda (2002) also believes that the increasing level of inequality in the treatment of employees will lead to the eventual loss of importance of this instrument. As outlined in the diary entries, companies were previously expected to guarantee to those employees who had no future in career development in their original company that they would be able to transfer on favorable terms. However, companies arrived at a situation where they could no longer uphold this promise for every employee, and it was difficult for them to justify differences in the treatment of employees. The diary entries support this view, showing how giving this opportunity to some, while others had to retire early or transfer permanently to another company, led to envy and perceptions of being treated unfairly.

While some companies have been carrying out large scale transfers of employees, transfers still have their limitations in terms of the number of employees involved, especially, as has been pointed out above, with transfers becoming more difficult in general.

15 September 2002 – On the way home I stopped for dinner at a Yakiniku restaurant close to my house where by coincidence I met a junior of mine who had recently left the company. Under the current conditions not every person is taken care of. He had not managed to obtain an order for transfer, and, as a result, had to retire early. Now, it seems that he has to attend a vocational training school. This is quite awful.[16]

Many Japanese corporations have moved one step up on the restructuring ladder and have carried out large scale workforce reductions. However, in so doing they have faced concerns about public image and legitimacy as well as legal restrictions concerning selective dismissals. Consequently, they have had to resort to an alternative – large scale voluntary early retirement exercises.

3.2   Retiring early, being retired, surviving

Early retirement exercises are often viewed as a benevolent alternative to selective dismissals. However, this does not mean that they are unproblematic for employers or employees. Voluntary early retirement exercises differ from selective dismissals or transfers in the sense that an employer usually offers all employees in a certain age range the choice to retire early. To entice employees to accept, employers offer a retirement package that usually includes significantly increased retirement allowances.

Yet, this procedure leaves companies with some uncertainties. Due to the voluntary nature of this method companies cannot know in advance which employees will take up the offer to retire early. However, as will be shown, many firms have not been willing to accept this situation and have tried to selectively influence certain employees to retire early.

Faced with the possibility of retiring early, employees have found themselves in a situation where they were forced to think about their future career and life course. In this respect employees had not only to consider their own prospects within and outside their current employment but also had to assess their current employer's future prospects given the fact that the reduction of the workforce often signals a corporate crisis. Thus early retirement programs regularly captured the minds of blog writers and writers' thoughts revolved around the following four main issues.

- Were early retirement programs really of a voluntary nature?
- Who was making use of early retirement programs – capable or less capable employees?
- How did employees who remained in the company react to early retirement exercises?
- What consequences did early retirement measures have on work patterns?

The first point to be taken up here is the way in which early retirement programs have been conducted. While participation in these programs has, in principle, been voluntary there has also been a tradition in many Japanese corporations to give certain employees a "tap on the shoulder" signaling to them that it is time to retire before reaching the official retirement age.

> *7 July 2000 – Our company has from last year on, or even earlier, used a so-called early retirement system, and somehow older men have received the tap on the shoulder: "Don't you want to retire quietly with an extra retirement allowance?" Such an older man was in our section, and at the end of this month he will retire....Nowadays, it is really the merit principle that counts, so it cannot be helped. Nonetheless, this older man is already between 50 and 55, I believe, and he is not married. In this situation, several problems might occur.*[17]

The next writer details his own encounter with company representatives.

> *6 June 2002 – Today, directors came around for interviews to outline the early retirement measures. Of course, at the moment I am not thinking of leaving the company. Since last year all the companies in our group have been in a very serious condition, and, as in many other companies, this has led to invitations to retire early. Interviews are conducted individually, employee by employee, to find out whether they are willing or not. By the way, I was told that if I retired right away I would receive 3.8 million yen in retirement allowance and that unemployment insurance payments would amount to an additional one million yen if I made use of the maximum period of half a year. What is this? For such an amount, under the current conditions how can you give up your job so carelessly? "I am not thinking about early retirement at all," I answered. As long as one cannot be forcibly discharged, I will stick to my job as long as I want to stick to it, especially since my first child will be born soon...The interview lasted one and a half hours so by that time the work day was already nearly over.*[18]

The next writer confirms the notion of companies actively targeting certain employees for early retirement and in this process resorting to various means.

> *30 November 2001 – The recruitment activities for the early retirement system came to an end today. Yet, the personnel department had*

decided to conduct individual interviews in advance, and therefore the deadline had no real meaning. Somehow or other, men and women aged 50 years and above seem to have responded. If one considers retirement allowances and payout of pensions, it might have been just in time for them.[19]

The next writer also describes pressure being exerted, with management even indicating to employees the possibility of selective dismissals under less favorable retirement conditions.

2 November 1999 – Company N [name provided in the diary] has announced a large restructuring program recently, and this time they seem to be using a different approach to previous initiatives used to reduce personnel ... I worked for a company that was affiliated with N previously so I became quite interested in the restructuring program, contacted a few acquaintances, and got several replies.

With the introduction of the early retirement system, people who retire early will receive a higher retirement allowance (about one year of wages). However, if one does not retire of one's own accord, or if it is judged that one is not helpful this time one will be retired forcibly by the company (previously by whatever means one retired it was always called resignation). Naturally, in this case one will receive no more retirement money than the tear of a sparrow.[20]

Within this notion, diary writers also showed skepticism in regard to the rhetoric used by companies to describe and justify their downsizing efforts, not readily accepting differences between the new programs and the traditional tap on the shoulder.

3 August 2001 – A leading manufacturer, who in the past did not resort to the practice of asking people to retire early by tapping them on the shoulder, has made a bold move towards the following. The company has not introduced dismissals by implementing a so-called favorable early retirement program, but instead calls it a program for the development of the next career. While it has been given a name that implies more, it is certainly aimed at reducing personnel by a tap on the shoulder. It targets people aged 45 and older, and a 50-year-old employee will receive more than 30 months of salary payment.[21]

Another writer described himself as being partly responsible for forcing some of his co-workers into early retirement and describes his feelings under the title *A System That Delivers Happiness.*

> *31 May 2002 – Today we had a farewell party after work. Someone from the same department, someone who has done me a lot of good, has, without reason, invited me to his farewell party. This person has made use of the currently popular early retirement system at our H factory and has retired five years before the regular retirement age, meaning he had to retire early. No, there was no way he could have avoided retirement.*

> *The main reason for this happening has been me. Because, over the last year, I have participated in the introduction of the A system for administrative reform, people have lost their jobs. In short, this A system has been so effective that the number of people having to leave the company has increased. While in the past these excess people would still have been put to use by redeploying their efforts into the development of new products, in times of economic crisis all of them have become the focus of restructuring...*

> *In the speeches that were made, the matter of the A system was raised: "Because of the introduction of the A-system," "If the A-system had not been there..., a little longer." I sat straight through these speeches and have taken them firmly into my heart word for word. Then I made a sincere pledge: I will create systems that bring happiness. I will never forget today's farewell party.*[22]

Another major theme that frequently appears in the diaries concerns the question of who is leaving the company. Here several writers express the view that mostly "capable" people with alternatives outside the companies leave while the "less capable" or those without initiative stay behind. Many writers link this notion with thoughts about how companies will cope with this outflow of people, and some even worry about the future of their companies.

> *17 March 2002 – There are also many early retirees; people who receive an increased retirement allowance and resign. While the system is supposedly for middle-aged employees who work poorly, many middle-aged employees who are doing well are also leaving. In addition, there are younger people who are not eligible for retirement but still resign.*[23]

A very similar statement is made by another writer who first outlines the financial consequences of the early retirement program introduced in his company before expressing his concerns about the future of the company after capable people decided to leave.

> *17 April 2002 – In the company from which I was originally transferred many people of the rank of department head and section head are retiring. They will be paid a retirement allowance ... plus a premium? An additional income will be paid out for two years. Calculated on a low basis, every person will receive 10 million yen, and since there are 30 people involved this will cost the company 300 million yen. Because many people above section head will retire, I think that this sum will be much higher. The normal way of thinking is (at least from my point of view) that those people who the company needs will leave, and those people the company does not need will stay. If this is really so, our company is in real danger.*[24]

And yet another such comment:

> *20 January 2000 – Because business is bad our company, too, has introduced an early retirement system. In short, since it has been regarded as pathetic to retire just like that after a tap on the shoulder, the company says 'let's increase the retirement payment a bit.' I suppose it is really the same story for every company where such a wicked practice has been introduced. Unfortunately, not only people who one really wants to retire, but also excellent people are flowing out. One after another people first receive a sizable sum of retirement money and then continue to progress in their careers. Our department too, has many such people.*[25]

With capable people purportedly having made use of early retirement programs, the question frequently came up of why companies would let such people go, or why companies accept applications by everyone interested in leaving even when the number of applications exceeds the number of employees originally targeted. In the following excerpt the diary writer provides his own explanation, arguing that companies basically regard the relationship with an employee as broken beyond repair once an employee has expressed the desire to leave the company.

> *9 April 2002 – At Hitachi 4,000 people were targeted for early retirement. However, they have registered interest from 9,000 people, and*

how can it be that they appear to be sending all those who are interested into early retirement. Uh, how can this be a good decision? Among those people, there have to be excellent ones. However, it is next to impossible to bring back a mind that has already broken away from the company. Even if one had restrained them, I sense that there would be no mutual relationship any longer. For good or for bad, my company has not been in this position. If it had been, what would have happened?[26]

Another writer contradicted the popular notion that older workers do not contribute enough to the company and are of no value. He also took up a point that will be addressed later in more detail – the departure from the company of older people who played an important role in socializing with and educating younger employees.

20 March 2002 – Yesterday was the farewell party for my very first supervisor. The people who were around at the time when I joined the company are leaving one by one and I feel somewhat lonely after all. Well, they have been harshly labeled as awful window sitters by some. Our workplace, however, is different from the financial sector and is an expert field where one carefully matures.[27]

The high retirement allowances offered in Japanese companies resulted in some uncertainty among employees who decided to remain with their companies despite being offered the chance to retire early. Employees who decided not to take up the offer asked themselves whether they had made the right decision by not applying, whether the company would be able to recover or whether the situation would even get worse and finally whether the same benefits would still be available by the time they would want or have to retire.

22 April 2002 – Today, I was handed a letter that stated: if you retire early "Your retirement payment..." It also gave an estimate of a gratuity payment. I am worried about whether I will still receive the same amount when I reach retirement age, or a lower amount. At the moment, I cannot imagine life without work; maybe this is something for other people.[28]

Another writer is also unsure about the true character of those retiring and asked whether it is a lack of aspiration that leads to their decision to retire or just the opposite – great foresight about the future development of the company.

> *4 March 2002 – Early retirement system interview: While I am not in the targeted age group and therefore not affected, this seems to be a scheme where you can retire comfortably in a fairly advantageous way. The general perception is that with anxiety about the future increasing, this is good for people who have no aspirations. At the same time it comes to one's mind that later someone might eventually state with a big laugh: "That K [person] had a lot of foresight, ha-ha-ha!" Gloomy feelings!*[29]

However, another employee expresses his astonishment about a colleague who gave up his job without having even secured a new position.

> *20 January 2000 – Even so, I was still amazed about a mail I received today from a 46-year-old man. It said: "Since it has come to my mind to finally change the course of my life I will take the risk." Without having secured new employment he resigned; it seems that he resigned first and only then began to look for new work. With countless companies showing bad results, one has to say farewell to the calm life where one just enters a company listed in the first section of the stock exchange and starts upon a career path. Still, it is amazing to take the decision to throw all this away, to enter into a totally unknown world, moreover, to step forward into a situation one does not understand.*[30]

Finally, a diary writer expresses deep concerns about the situation in his company and is disturbed by the fact that other people could make the decision to leave the company so easily while he was not confident enough to draw the necessary conclusions himself.

> *28 June 2001 – After work was finished we had a farewell party for early retirees. Because our company is in a slump, wages and bonuses have been cut, and the coffers are in a desolate state. In this situation, a favorable early retirement exercise was carried out. When the company recruited retirees, quite a number of people raised their arms. Today was the farewell party for two of them. If such a number of people raise their hands, the future prospects of the company are surely bleak. But, if I retired, I would not be confident I could feed myself. I cannot retire.*[31]

Early retirement programs have often targeted workers in their forties and fifties, and, as many writers reported, the retirement of these
people was disruptive to the networks of human relationships that
existed in companies. This has already been touched upon in some
of the previous excerpts, with the following writers reiterating such
sentiments.

> *1 August 2000 – On the 31st of July, the notice listing changes of
> personnel was put up. In addition to the usual transfers, we had a
> column on early retirements. There were people included who at the
> time I joined the company had kindly taught me several things about
> how to prepare to be a business man. If society becomes like this, the
> satisfaction of being a salaryman will surely come to an end. I would
> regret this.*[32]

However, there are also accounts of direct consequences in the workplace itself, apart from the break-up of relationships and the perception that some capable people were leaving. The following writer
complains about the increased workload due to the reduction of
personnel.

> *12 November 2002 – Lately, at my workplace, there have been quite
> a number of early retirees and I have been feeling somewhat lonely.
> In this situation, it is not as if the remaining people were blessed with
> happiness – the amount of work has increased. It can be called "restruc-
> turing share"; while one cannot say that the work load has doubled, we
> now have to work 1.2 to 1.5 times as much. Suddenly, all this came to
> my mind at work today.*[33]

In her diary entry below a writer voiced similar concerns:

> *19 January 2004 – Compared to last year, work has increased by 10%
> this year and there seems to be a trend in which personnel costs are
> tightened by reducing the number of employees as much as possible. Is
> this restructuring? (tears). If I resign, there is the possibility that those
> around me will also resign. At the moment we are operating with barely
> enough people. If just one person takes any extra leave, it immediately
> leads to a big panic. You are still increasing the workload and further
> reducing the number of people? Boss!*[34]

There are only very few accounts available written by people who have actually retired. One of the few writers in this category expresses his feelings very clearly and in this process even points to general differences he perceives in the attitudes towards retirement between Europe and Japan.

> *8 February 2001 – I will finally retire in 39 days. With this recession, I thought that I would bring the date for retirement forward a little. Just a little ... But, if I had continued to work another year, next year about this time, I think I would have had the same feelings. Europeans have a retirement party and it seems that they celebrate retirement. If Japanese retire, they shed tears as they have lost their work. What about these differences? ... Having retired early, I feel like a person without a nationality ... Oh dear!*[35]

Finally, a statement that is different from the previous accounts in that it has a more forward looking nature; the writer asking how his company will be able to eventually recover from the early retirement exercise.

> *25 January 2000 – It seems that the preparatory session titled "meeting to explain the early retirement system" is coming closer. X thousand workers are targeted and it seems that interviews will also be conducted if necessary. This is happening in every company and is not uncommon at all, but if our organization develops such an environment, it will be very tough ... What seeds of recovery will we have to nurture so that this will not happen again? Well, all we can do is to exert ourselves to improve the short-term and medium-term results.*[36]

As for transfers, efforts have been made to explore the phenomenon of early retirement in a quantitative manner and results largely support the opinions and perceptions voiced by diary writers. The Japanese Institute of Labor Policy and Training conducted a large scale survey in regard to the reorganization of corporations in January 2002 and in this process collected 1,683 answers from companies with more than 30 employees, and 2,693 answers from regular employees who had gone through the experience of changing companies within the previous year (JIL 2002).

Among the employees surveyed were 124 people who had responded to early retirement programs. The results are biased in the sense that only people who had managed to find new positions as regular employees were surveyed. The results show that the announcement of early retirement programs can indeed be the initial factor that leads to employees thinking about their future since 53.7% of employees had not thought about giving up their positions before the program was announced, and unlike the 38% that had, might not have left the company otherwise (n=82). Employees seemed to have been quite confident about their future with 43.5% having left their former employers without having secured a new job (n=124).

It is difficult to assess to what degree people rationalized their reasons for taking up early retirement. Still, reasons given by respondents support the perceptions voiced by blog writers. Survey respondents showed themselves as being largely of a proactive mindset, with only a minority admitting to pressures. From the multiple-choice answers available the most popular reason was "uncertainty about the future of the company" (38.7%), followed by "it was a good opportunity to challenge myself in a new job" (37.9%), "favorable circumstances" (27.4%), "because the company encouraged me to do so" (25%), "not having succeeded in my previous company" (21%), "working conditions in regard to wage or retirement allowance had worsened or were expected to do so" (20.2%), "the possibility of utilizing my own skills within the company had disappeared" (12.1%), "if I had not responded I would have become the target of selective dismissal" (5.6%) and finally "I did not want to burden the company by staying" (3.2%) (JIL 2002: 21).

In their blogs, employees also related perceived effects on companies such as the outflow of valuable people, effects on their own or their colleagues' morale, or the deterioration of personal relationships, and it is hard to imagine that companies have not thought about such factors when planning downsizing exercises. The perspectives of companies on the consequences of early retirement programs were captured in two surveys. The first survey was carried out as part of a JIL study. It asked companies about the effects of downsizing and differentiated these effects by the methods used to implement personnel reductions, with methods ranging from relatively indirect ones such as natural attrition to harsher measures such as dismissals (Table 3.4). Looking at the results, more than 50% of responding companies recorded a decrease in morale among their employees and interestingly, this occurred regardless of the method applied. Concerning early retirement, the survey reinforced the impression

Table 3.4 Effects of downsizing by method (multiple answers, in %)

Downsizing method	Drop in morale	Increased work load	Increased productivity	Loss of valuable personnel	Increase of employee initiated resignations	Decreased productivity	Increase in morale	Problems in recruiting
Total (n=874)	51.5	45.8	35.9	33.0	17.2	14.3	13.6	11.3
Suppress new hiring (672)	54.9	47.8	36.9	33.6	16.5	14.7	12.9	13.1
Natural attrition (713)	52.2	47.3	36.2	33.6	16.5	14.7	12.9	11.5
Transfers (227)	59.5	54.2	32.2	37	15.9	16.3	14.1	11.9
Early retirement exercises (299)	59.2	46.2	32.8	50.5	17.4	16.4	13	10.0
Dismissals (60)	68.3	38.3	23.3	38.3	16.7	28.3	8.3	18.3
Reduction in number of non-regular employees (260)	57.3	37.3	33.8	33.8	16.5	23.5	11.5	14.2

Source: JIL 2002.

that companies lost valuable personnel, the scores of other methods being significantly lower in this category.

Another survey that looked more deeply into the workings of early retirement programs was the Survey of Labor Administration. It asked employers about the consequences and their perceptions of early retirement programs (Table 3.5). The results show that retirement

Table 3.5 Consequences of early retirement exercises as perceived by companies (multiple answers, in %)

Company size by no. of employees	Total	> 5000	1000–4999	300–999	100–299	30–99
Early retirement exercises resulted in:						
Adjustment of personnel	56.5	78.4	59.4	48.7	57.0	57.4
Promotion of organizational renewal	36.8	30.7	43.1	35.0	40.8	34.3
Productivity improvements	11.0	25.0	15.0	10.3	11.6	10.1
Reduction of costs	80.2	83.0	83.3	82.2	80.7	79.0
Improvement of morale	4.9	2.3	5.0	2.3	0.8	8.0
Increased proportion of younger workers	8.1	9.1	6.1	4.6	9.4	8.5
Outflow of crucial personnel	22.5	21.6	41.5	21.2	25.3	18.8
Decrease of productivity	4.3	2.3	11.9	5.9	6.0	2.0
Deterioration of morale	11.6	8.0	14.7	13.4	13.2	9.9
Deterioration of interpersonal relationships	2.7	–	3.5	1.1	3.5	2.7
Increase of work hours for remaining workers	23.9	21.6	25.0	22.7	24.0	24.0
Other	1.8	1.1	4.8	1.1	3.7	0.5
No effect	7.6	8.0	6.1	8.8	5.3	8.9
No answer	1.1	2.3	2.0	–	0.5	1.5

Source: Kōsei Rōdō Daijin Kanbō Tōkei Jōhōbu (2001).

exercises for most companies clearly led to a reduction of costs, for a majority of companies to an adjustment of the numbers of their employees, and for a significant number of companies to a reinforcement of measures for organizational renewal. Concerning negative effects, a number of companies cited the outflow of crucial personnel as well as an increase in working hours for remaining employees. Effects in regard to morale and productivity seemed to be less significant, but again showed the complexity of the issue addressed. While some companies perceived a decrease in morale and an increase in productivity, others saw decreases or increases in both areas.

Overall, Japanese employees reported that stress in their workplaces increased and uncertainty about the future of workplaces and the company in general played an important role in contributing to increased levels of stress. In response to a survey conducted by the Japanese Institute of Labor Policy and Training in January 2004 nearly half of the respondents said they felt that stress had increased in their workplaces over the previous three years (23.4% significantly and 26.8% somewhat). Others, however, reported no change (23.2%), lower stress levels (5.3%) or even significantly lower stress levels (3.2%), or could not answer the question because they had not been in the company for long (16.8%). For male employees this number was even higher with 56.8% reporting significantly higher or higher stress levels. The same applied for regular employees where 57.1% saw higher stress levels (JILPT 2004b). Looking at the factors underlying the increased stress levels, anxieties about the company and the workplace ranked prominently with 28.2% and 22.7% of respondents naming these factors (Table 3.6).

3.3   Downsizing and restructuring in context

The larger discussion on downsizing and restructuring activities in Japan should begin with an overview of the legal situation. Until the year 2003 the dismissal of workers was not specifically regulated in the labor laws apart from the fact that employers had to give employees a certain period of notice. However, even then the situation was largely regulated through court decisions, which made dismissals difficult since courts regularly interpreted selective dismissals as an abuse of rights and of a superior position as stipulated in the Civil Code. To establish whether rights were abused courts

Table 3.6 Factors leading to stress in the workplace (multiple answers in %)

Factors	Total	Men	Regular employees
Future of company	28.2	33.4	31.8
Heavy responsibility	25.4	29.7	27.6
Large amount of work	25.4	27.5	27.0
Security of employee's own workplace	22.7	18.6	17.3
Long working hours	22.7	27.5	25.2
Bad workplace relationships	18.0	13.9	16.9
Bad workplace environment	14.2	11.5	13.9
No one to turn to for advice	13.8	12.8	14.3
Many irregular tasks	30.0	16.2	14.2
Work content does not fit	12.5	11.5	13.3
Work results become important	11.8	15.2	13.2
Difficult to keep up with advances in technology	10.3	11.0	10.8
Overload of information	8.0	9.3	9.0
Competition with colleagues	1.2	1.0	1.3

Note: Responses from 1,066 companies, 7,288 employees, for above item 5,934 employees.
Source: JILPT 2004b.

regularly checked four provisions: "whether reduction in the workforce was truly needed; whether the employer has made an effort to avoid dismissals; whether the selection of people to be dismissed was made rationally; and whether the employer had provided an explanation to the workers and the labor unions and discussed the matter with them in an effort to obtain their understanding" (Nakakubo 2004: 13). Only in 2003 was an article on dismissals added to the Labor Standards Law stating that: "A dismissal shall be considered an abuse of the right to dismiss and therefore null and void if it is not based on objectively reasonable grounds and may not be recognized as socially acceptable" (Article 18–2). While some have argued that this codification restricts employers in their ability to dismiss employees more than in the past, Nakakubo (2004) argues that this is not the case and that the main effect might instead be the fact that employees become more aware of their rights and do not just accept dismissals.

Apart from the legal aspect, the social acceptance of downsizing measures also needs to be discussed. The following chapter will discuss the issue of so-called long-term or even lifetime employment in more detail. This assured many Japanese employees – that they could spend most of their career with one company. Companies have tried by all means to avoid dismissals and companies dismissing employees were normally seen as being in a real state of crisis. Efforts of companies to reduce their labor forces might therefore not only damage the basic foundations of understanding between employees and employers but also tarnish the reputation of the company with other stakeholders such as investors, customers, lenders, and suppliers, who assume that a company would only resort to such measures when forced to do so by severe financial distress (Usui and Colignon 1996, Genda and Rebick 2000). The legal situation and larger social legitimacy concerns explain why Japanese companies resorted to inter-company transfers and voluntary early retirement exercises, and also why companies offered relatively high amounts of compensation to employees that accepted offers of early retirement.

The diary accounts as well as the survey results can be further discussed within the general literature on downsizing practices. So-called downsizing became a popular topic of academic debate in the wake of the so-called first round of corporate downsizing within the depressed US economy of the early 1980s. Interest increased later when it became clear that companies had discovered downsizing as a tool to not only counter cyclical drops in demand but also to regularly achieve cost reductions, general improvements in profitability, and competitiveness. Downsizing exercises were pursued to achieve structural changes in workforces and in that regard they increasingly targeted white-collar employees (Capelli 1999).

The consequences and processes of downsizing have been investigated from a variety of perspectives, among them societal, ethical, economical and managerial. A major issue within this discussion concerns the effects of the various downsizing measures on those employees who do not leave but remain behind.

Kuzmits and Sussman have treated early retirement largely as a policy option of companies versus the alternative of forced discharges (layoffs) and overall they see only a minimal impact of early retirement programs upon organizational culture and climate. The situation in Japan differed however. Japanese companies could not choose whether to introduce an early retirement exercise or to conduct the large scale selective dismissal of employees. Early retirement exercises that in the US appeared still as a benevolent measure compared to layoffs, were considered a harsh measure in Japan, and surveys as well as diary accounts do show an impact on organizational culture and climate. This might however, also be due to the way in which early retirement programs were executed, with surveys and diary entries showing that Japanese corporations exerted pressure on employees in order to reach the quantitative and qualitative objectives of their downsizing exercises.

Rosenblatt and Schaeffer (2000) have summarized the effects of downsizing exercises. First they note high levels of stress in the organization based on factors such as the decision makers' frustration and disillusionment, since downsizing is often viewed as a business failure in a growth-biased environment. Stress is aggravated through a loss of human and social capital, with skills disappearing and the organizational memory being disrupted. In addition, shifts in organizational structure lead to unbalanced workloads and people see losses and separation in relationships. Employees might be alienated by the sudden curtailment of available information, and overall the psychological contract between company and employee might dissolve, with employees feeling betrayed due to their strong sense of ownership and entitlement to their jobs.

Diary entries and surveys show that all these effects occurred in Japanese organizations. Employees felt poorly informed about decisions being made, saw their workloads increasing and changing, and also experienced loss of relationships. Appelbaum, Close and Klasa (1999) noted that many organizations offer supportive measures for employees selected for dismissal, but do not really assess the effects these measures might have on those who stay behind. They summarized the variety of feelings and reactions of workers staying behind in the companies under the term "survivor syndrome." Littler (2000) has identified six human resource variables that point to the existence of survivor syndrome in organizations: decreased employee morale, decreased employee motivation, decreased employee commitment to the organization, decreased employee job satisfaction, increased concern about job security, and decreased promotion opportunities within the organization. Finally, Spreitzer and Mishra (2000) proposed four survivor archetypes: "walking wounded" who respond to organizational downsizing with fear, "faithful followers" who largely regard measures as benign, "carping critics" who respond cynically

to measures and might even be destructive, and finally "active advo-
cates" who are optimistic about events, feel they can cope with them
and show an overall constructive attitude.   *Survivor syndrome*

Diary entries as well as survey results show that symptoms of "survivor syndrome" occurred in Japanese organizations. Concerning
the earlier mentioned categorization by Spreitzer and Mishra, most
Japanese diary writers that have experienced downsizing seem to fall
into the category of walking wounded by showing increased insecurity about their own future in the company and not feeling suffi-
ciently equipped to handle ongoing events. Those who commented
on early retirement measures from the outside can be categorized as
carping critics, seeing the current restructuring measures as a break
in trust and going against all established practices of management
in Japan.

The diary excerpts have shown that transfers and early retirement
programs potentially have lasting effects on personal relationships
in Japanese corporations. Matanle argued that relationships form a
constituting role in Japanese workplaces, and do so more than in
Western organizations. Employees value relationships and derive
part of their work satisfaction from the fact that they are able and
capable of fulfilling responsibilities that arise from such relationships. Based on the work by Plath and his own research, Matanle
(2003: 145) argued that

> many Japanese employees undoubtedly possess a deep appreciation
> of their roles and obligations within the complex web of relationships
> that constitute their lives. Moreover, they are actually concerned about
> fulfilling these roles and relationships, not so much out of a reluctant
> sense of duty, but because these aspects of their lives are valued for
> their potential to enhance social life in an integrated and synergis-
> tic manner...Thus lifetime membership of the corporate community,
> although it may not result in the most individually fulfilling life, and
> may be somewhat of a disappointment if that is the case, is valued pri-
> marily for the relational synergies and opportunities that are unleashed
> by such a system.

Restructuring activities of Japanese corporations thus did not only
directly disrupt interpersonal relationships, with people having to
leave the company, but as the blog entries have shown, also deprived

employees from fulfilling what they perceived as their own obligations, such as taking good care of employees with whom they had
been entrusted or by showing their appreciation for favors received
in the past. Based on the argument by Matanle on the importance
of relationships, one can assume a deep influence of restructuring
activities on the morale and motivation of employees in Japanese
corporations.

A very important point that is not addressed in the literature and
surveys, but that becomes very clear through diary entries is that
in the process of voluntary early retirement exercises all employees
in an organization are affected by being forced to reflect about and
to make decisions about their own future. In making this decision
employees have to consider a variety of issues such as plans for their
own future, employability outside the company, their financial situation, the future of their company in general and the outlook for
the company after the conclusion of early retirement exercises, especially since there is the perception that it is capable people who leave
the company in such circumstances. The substantial compensation
packages offered by companies have complicated the situation further. On the one hand these have established a certain legitimacy
of the measures with remaining employees by assuring them that
people who left the company were taken good care of; on the other
hand, they have caused anxiety for employees that decided to stay,
since they had to worry whether they had made the right decision to
stay behind. It has been shown that many employees who left their
companies only started to think about leaving when an early retirement exercise was announced. This being so, it can be expected that
in the wake of early retirement exercises even employees who stayed
behind became much more conscious about their own situation, the
situation of their company and the way it was managed.

From a management perspective a greater awareness by employees of the situation of the company might be desirable and might
even lead to higher productivity and work engagement. However,
by increasing anxiety companies are walking a fine line and therefore have to assure employees continuously that their efforts are
being recognized and rewarded (Hunter 2003, Brockner et al. 1992).
However, so far, Japanese corporations have focused on long-term
rewards and might therefore be unable to counter daily anxieties
that arise in restructuring situations.

Cascio argued for the US that downsizing has "exploded the myth of job security" and thereby changed the conditions of the "psychological contract that binds workers to organizations" (Cascio 1993: 103). Similarly, the increased awareness of Japanese employees in regard to the uncertainties of their workplaces might have a lasting effect, with companies only feeling the consequences once the Japanese economic situation has picked up and more employment opportunities become available again. As was outlined earlier, Capelli (1999) reported that in the US employees drew their own conclusions from the restructuring exercises of the 1980s. They not only increased their own efforts to acquire skills that guaranteed them employability outside their own companies but also showed more willingness to leave their companies when more employment opportunities opened up again. Thus, corporations emerged from the period of restructuring with less control over their employees than they had previously when employment was seen by employees as long-term and stable.

Whether such a situation will materialize in Japan cannot be determined at the moment. Much depends on what stance Japanese corporations take towards downsizing in the future. If they see downsizing just as a measure to apply in situations of corporate crisis, employment relationships might not change permanently. However, as has been pointed out, many US corporations have come to see periodic downsizing exercises as a valuable tool to keep organizations efficient and slim, and have increasingly resorted to this instrument in times when organizations were profitable and showed no apparent signs of crisis. Ogishi (2006) also points to the fact that among the companies instituting reorganization measures in Japan there have been some that were under no actual pressure to do so.

Hence Karake-Shalhoub (1999: 2) argues that companies need to find new ways to sustain the loyalty of their employees, and that one idea is to appeal to the self-interest of employees.

Downsizing has changed the ways in which companies and their employees relate. Traditionally, loyalty was rewarded with security. However, with many organizations downsizing, they are no longer able or willing to guarantee lifelong employment. When companies downsize and lay off employees, they expect the remaining employees to pull together for the common good. Instead, companies often discover that employees have become suspicious and less productive. When employees feel less loyal, they focus on protecting self-interest rather than on working for the good of the firm. To channel that self-interest or benefit the firm, managers can create a contract of mutual commitment between themselves and employees. In the contract, the manager commits to helping employees achieve personal goals, and employees commit to helping the manager attain the company's goals.

As already pointed out, restructuring measures run parallel to initiatives by companies to change or adapt the general principles of employment in Japanese corporations as well as changes in the composition of the workforce. Thus, the above questions should be kept in mind when discussing these issues in the following chapters.

4
Facing Changing
Principles of Employment

20 October 2004 – In October, my salary was raised. My company is old-fashioned so this was done based on the seniority system. Every year, the salary rises little by little. This is the basic salary, so the bonus also increases and I will enjoy this in winter. Moreover, even if my superior changes or overtime is paid to the fullest, nothing is said. While I can get it, I will take it. Yosh, I will buy a new car next year![37]

17 November 2004 – When still at an age before my skin got wrinkled, I recklessly spouted: "I quickly want to be older than 30!" Then, at work, no matter how heavy the responsibility, I, who had no title on my name card, was treated like a young fool by clients who were old men. So I lamented "It would be good to be in a managerial position, but since our company runs a seniority-based system there is no way to get there before the age of 30." So I declared: "I want to be 30 quickly!" But now that I have passed 30 "I want to return to youth" (hello there!).[38]

27 July 2004 – Today I turned 32. When looking for your first job, did you all plan what kind of job and what kind of life you would lead? When I was looking for work, it was the peak of the bubble period when "lifetime employment" and the "seniority-based system" were taken for granted, so I thought that I would lead a safe life at my workplace. I entrusted my life to the company.[39]

The writers of the above three blog excerpts take up different aspects of work under the principles of lifelong employment, seniority payment and advancement. The first writer expresses his joy at the fact that his company still applies seniority principles in remuner- ating its workforce; the second writer, while somewhat vainly prais- ing the advantages of youth, shows how seniority has an effect on everyday work in Japanese corporations, and finally the third writer remembers the expectations he had when taking up his first job.

At first sight, blog entries that refer to lifetime employment and seniority, which are the long standing, overarching principles of work and employment in Japan, suggest a generational gap in per- ceptions in terms of aspirations and expectations. However, taking a closer look at this situation, especially in regard to the introduction of performance-oriented systems of pay and advancement, shows that opinions are also split within generations. While many blog writers welcome the introduction of new incentive systems, others voice anxieties. However, writers largely agree that changes will be lasting and will thereby necessitate a change of mindset. Indeed, many employees seem to have drawn their own conclusions and report that they are striving for more independence in building their careers.

The following narrative of perceptions of blog writers concerning lifetime employment, seniority and incentive systems largely follows the order of the above argument by first showing perceived gener- ational differences, then outlining the discussion surrounding the introduction of performance-based principles in remuneration and advancement, and finally looking at the way blog writers portray their responses to the new situation. As for the previous chapter, the picture drawn from blogs will be contrasted with additional materials to further substantiate or qualify findings.

4.1   Responding to change: generations apart?

> *27 September 2002 – My successor is of a higher rank, and not just that, he had already been in charge of this task for several years before I took over. In the end, he just created confusion. He gets paid a higher salary than me so he should work accordingly. Bubble employees are really useless...I think the company once recruited many people like this; irresponsible and only good at talking. Aren't they embarrassed to ask subordinates questions about work? Not only that, they ask many times about the same*

thing. I had to work until after 10 pm at night and still did not get my own work done.[40]

The above writer chose the term "bubble employee" to describe an employee who began his career during the period of the bubble economy. Indeed, during the few years of the bubble economy Japanese companies expecting further rapid growth brought in large numbers of employees who were often lured with grand promises for future careers and rewards. Not surprisingly, these employees suffered the envy and scorn of employees that joined the company in a different situation.

5 February 2004 – My generation experienced the bubble era during our schooldays and started working right after the bubble burst, and so is a generation that was shaped during tough times without such things as bonuses and so on. The seniors are what we call "bubble employees" and there are many people who just had good luck, without real ability; but compared to us they have weak spots. Just when my generation began to work, the seniority system deteriorated and was replaced by the results-oriented-system.[41]

The above statement also explains the malicious joy that the next writer expressed after seeing "bubble employees" becoming the target of restructuring measures.

27 November 1999 – Now the ones suffering most seem to be the bubble employees who are in their late twenties or early thirties. That era was an era when one could simply come to the company and do nothing but breathe. So, even if they had no ability they joined the company. It seems that this kind of person is increasingly becoming the target of restructuring. As for those of us from the job hunters' ice age, our nature and the way we think regarding the company is totally different ... What will you do, bubble employees?[42]

Some so-called "bubble employees" actually agree with their younger colleagues, but like the following writer, shift the blame to employers who had not prepared people for a different paradigm of work.

10 April 2000 – Time passed quickly, but it has been eight years since I started work. Eight years ago was the golden age of the bubble and it was entirely a seller's market. Well, it was reported on television that we are now in a hiring freeze. This is because the era's paradigm has changed. It is easy to look at it as if one is not concerned and say that these people are just unfortunate, but this change has affected not only job seekers but also the way of thinking of bubble employees like me. What surprised me after I entered the company was that it was an organization ignorant of other industries and lines of business. Probably the corporate culture was responsible? I still remember clearly that when I entered the company the then president proclaimed in regard to people who had left the company: "No one has succeeded after leaving this company." Well nowadays, there are many instances where people who changed jobs clearly moved upwards. Without doubt my era can be called a turning point.[43]

The following writer also describes himself as largely unprepared for the new challenges, and even feels compelled to provide justification for having stayed with his company for so long. Whether he exaggerates or not, he recounts a popular anecdote about a middle-aged job interviewee to illustrate the way that Japanese companies encouraged employees to build careers as generalists and neglected the development of individual skills.

11 May 2004 – When I came into this company I actually entered under the assumption "Let's assume 10 years." I did not expect to leave within three years, but I also did not expect to obstinately stay all my life...But, I think that one needs to judge what happened from the perspective of that time. During that time I married and had children, and maybe, while it appeared as if one could not resign because there was no choice, one did get to feel more and more comfortable, and taking the risk of resigning just appeared too troublesome. There is also the age issue. And in addition, if one has just spent the days idling around, one has neither the motivation nor technical skills to develop along a new path...As has often been said, when asked during a job interview "What are you able to do?" desolate middle-aged men answer "I can be section chief or department head." That is all that there is to their existence.[44]

However, generational conflicts exist between all age groups and not just between those who began their careers during and after the bubble economy. Writing in 1999, an author held the baby boomer generation (born in the late 1940s) responsible for causing the problems of the bubble economy by denying those who joined later a say in corporate matters.

> *5 October 1999 – What is a "bubble employee?" Well, since I joined the company in 1988, I have belonged to what the mass media calls the "bubble employee" generation. In this severe recession, our generation is often singled out, but I am not happy with what has been said, so here I will present a rebuttal. Well, over these last 2–3 years, many famous big companies have suddenly collapsed, but to begin with it is the "baby boomer generation" that is currently in charge of decision making in companies. Speaking frankly, just when my generation has finally taken over management jobs, we are not in the position to say this and that about the company policy ... It makes no sense to judge whether our generation of bubble employees is inferior in regard to ability or not, and I am angry that in this way a specific generation is made scapegoats. What led to the present stupor is probably the baby boomers' indecisiveness. Isn't it because they do not want this to be pointed out that they came up with such a theory?*[45]

In their diary entries employees address a number of issues, many of which need further clarification and discussion. Younger diary writers frequently point to the difficulties they faced in securing a job, an experience that seems to have had an important influence on shaping their attitudes and perceptions in regard to colleagues who entered under more favorable conditions.

It has already been shown in the second chapter that Japanese corporations have changed the composition of their workforces and in this process have reduced the number of regular employees. The recruitment drive that Japanese corporations initiated during the bubble economy saw the number of regular employees increasing by 3.5 million between 1987 and 1992. Companies slightly increased the number of regular employees further by 400,000 until 1997, but afterwards their efforts to reduce employment kicked in, which led to a radical decrease by 4.9 million regular employees, bringing the figure back to the pre-bubble level (Table 2.1).

The prolonged restrictive hiring, however, left companies with an unbalanced age structure that through an adherence to seniority principles not only negatively affected the cost structure of companies but also the motivation of employees. Employees who had joined companies during the period of the bubble economy had expected to reach their first career milestone at age 35 to 39 by being promoted to management level (Nohara 1999). However, before they reached this age they found themselves not only competing for fewer advancement opportunities in a harsh economic climate, but also competing with younger employees who, through the introduction of performance-based incentive systems, were encouraged to challenge their older colleagues.

Statistics that compare the situations in 1990 and in 2003 show that to counter this situation companies exercised some leniency by creating new positions for their employees; the fact that a department manager was supervising about 35 staff in 1987 but only 26 staff in 2003 points in this direction. Nevertheless, far fewer employees of one cohort eventually reached management positions and even then, only after a longer period of tenure with their companies (JILPT 2005b). In 1990 33.3% of male employees in their early fifties with a high school degree were of the rank of general manager; however by 2003 this figure was down to only 20.8% (JILPT 2005b). Male employees also had to compete increasingly with female colleagues. While still at an overall low level, the share of female employees in management increased between 1990 and 2003 from 3.1 to 6.1%, with the number reaching 3.1% for department heads (general manager), 4.6% for section heads (managers) and 9.4% for assistant managers (JILPT 2005b).

Surveys show that employees of different age groups have varied perceptions of the core elements of Japanese employment such as lifelong employment and the application of seniority principles (Chart 4.1), with older employees showing a higher affinity for those principles. Yet, it can be assumed that differences in perceptions about seniority and lifelong employment always existed. Employees have always sought fast advancement at a younger age and thereby felt somewhat restricted by seniority principles, and only at a later stage in life learned to really appreciate the security that the two principles provided them with.

Chart 4.1 also shows that the number of people who appreciate lifetime employment is lower than those who appreciate seniority. Thus the drive of companies to replace seniority with merit-based principles

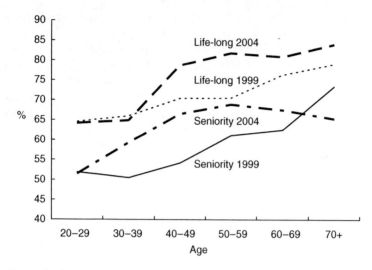

Chart 4.1 Opinions about lifelong employment and seniority (respondents with affirmative answers to the question: Is lifelong employment/seniority good?)

Note: Male employees by age group, August/September 2004, 4,000 employees (2,729 respondents), employees who answered "good" or "rather good."

Source: JILPT 2005a.

should have met with some appreciation by employees, and blog entries will demonstrate that to a certain degree this was indeed the case. Yet, there seems to have been a certain re-appreciation of seniority between 1999 and 2004. With merit-based incentive systems no longer just being a theoretical alternative, but having become the reality in many companies, this raises interesting questions about the way those principles were introduced in Japanese corporations and what consequences the application of the principles had in workplaces.

4.2 From seniority to performance

Online diary writers were split in their assessment of the introduction of performance-based pay systems, with some strongly demanding such a change, others strongly rejecting it, and some being undecided, mainly worrying about the way the principles were actually implemented.

The first blog entry is from a young female diary writer who describes her new work environment as being full of opportunities, expressing hope that the abolishment of seniority principles will allow her to advance regardless of gender or educational qualifications.

> *25 July 2004 – Therefore from tomorrow for one week, I will work hard to increase results (figures). I aim to become an assistant manager (group leader) next year. The era of the seniority system at work is over. It now depends on how much actual ability one has. Even if I am not respected as a woman, at least I hope for a fair assessment at work. Not on the basis of whether one is male, female, university-educated, high school graduate or vocational school graduate, but on the basis of actual ability.*[46]

The next writer, however, expresses disillusionment. Obviously he had been under the impression that his company already rewarded performance, but then found out that seniority still played a larger role. Consequently he criticizes the fact that actual work attitude and performance are not reflected properly in remuneration.

> *27 May 2004 – According to what I heard, whether an employee is clearly unable to do his work or cannot listen or one who is clearly special and is able to do his work and quick to catch on, one can say that the salary is almost the same. It seems that the salary gap based on seniority or the number of years of service remains strong. I really don't understand why the salary is the same for employees who simply stand around in a daze and hurried employees who don't take breaks in order to meet urgent pressing deadlines. What is the company thinking? I have come to think that I'm a fool for working seriously these three years. Definitely, from tomorrow I will take things easy.*[47]

Foreign-owned companies are often seen as front-runners in the introduction of performance-based principles in Japan. The following citation is by a student who encountered a distinctly different atmosphere when going for an interview in a foreign-owned company.

> *19 August 2004 – Today, I went for an interview with a certain foreign-owned company ... Arghh, I was surprised (laugh). It was the first time I*

had experienced the atmosphere of a foreign company; it was great (^-^). What is good? Isn't it good to matter-of-factly emphasize actual ability? Look, isn't business originally a matter-of-fact thing? One can control things by oneself...And, I greatly welcome emphasis on actual ability. It is far better than the seniority system. The next question is whether I have the skill to work in a foreign-owned company or not...Judgment will be passed. This is still in the future.[48]

Another blog writer supports this impression. She relates discrepancies in attitudes of salesmen to differences in employment principles, and criticizes the lack of qualifications of employees who have developed their careers as generalists under the seniority-oriented system.

26 May 2004 – Salesmen: I have received visits from salesmen from certain companies. Salesmen from various companies have come flying by. Since my boss has also received some of them I have not seen all of them, but from the perspective of a customer it looks like real competition and I feel that I can compare. They have to find out about our needs. The technique of asking and listening, making concrete propositions concerning our needs, technical knowledge. This is the stuff they should show off. In general, based on my subjective individual assessment, I have the feeling that foreign companies are excelling here because they build on results- and competence-oriented principles, do their business in English; an English/American-like culture has spread...I have the feeling that many salesmen of Japanese companies are doing their work as just their job, and are only in their position because age is regarded as important. They do not have the expected proper product knowledge, they are just begging, some of them don't even beg properly.[49]

However, many writers are not happy with the shift towards performance-oriented principles at their workplaces.

16 January 2002 – Work!! Work!! Work!! I looked at various diaries and recently there has been a lot about work!! Certainly, once one starts to work, a large part of one's life becomes work...I am still young, so things are fine, but there are quite a lot of worries about the future...Honestly, I think the seniority system is better than the ability-based system. Currently, I'm young so I am unlikely to be fired, so I'm fine, but concerning the future ... As one grows older, it is normal that one's bodily and mental strength will deteriorate. The only things that will increase are experience and body weight ... If one has a family and if the children grow older too, expenses will increase ... As for the working ability, it will fall ...[50]

While earlier on a diary writer appreciated a foreign company's emphasis on performance, another writer felt the opposite when attending a job interview. He conveys the idea that companies are pursuing the new principles with religious fervor.

23 June 2003 – Today I had a company briefing and the first interview. Talking about the outcome, I don't have a good feeling. For several reasons ... There are 10 applicants per position. But not only this. How should I describe it? I was shown a company video and it left a feeling of coldness. Not only that. It's not good to compare it to a new religion, but how else can I say it? It was said that under the results-oriented system one is evaluated purely for what one has achieved. I was shown a video with interviews of people, all of whom have succeeded. What about the people who have been weeded out? Basically, my own character is not suited to a company following the results-oriented or competence-oriented system. Currently, I want to work peacefully ... My aspiration is not to rise upwards, but to have security. That isn't bad, is it? It is a matter of values and life styles.[51]

Although only 28 years of age the writer of the next diary entry still worries whether he can cope in the new work environment. Again the issue of specific qualifications comes up, with the writer being unsure whether he can find a workplace in a less competitive industry.

29 March 2004 – Uneasiness breeds uneasiness – As usual my head is full of uneasiness about work. Whether one is a part-timer, full-timer, company employee, dispatch worker or contract worker ... If one has not really established oneself in one's work, it's hard to imagine what will happen after one turns 35. Probably I will not be able to cope with the "results-oriented system" that is being trumpeted loudly in our competitive society. If so, I don't know how I should live. That is, the experience I have accumulated so far can only be used in the fiercely competitive semi-conductor industry. However, eventually I ended up running away...Shall I choose a totally unrelated industry? Can a 28-year-old change his ways[52]

Feelings of anxiety are shared by a female employee who just started in her new job and concludes that in a performance-oriented environment she has to prioritize her own well-being, and that this will affect her interaction with colleagues.

6 September 2004 – In my new workplace my affiliation has not yet been decided and there has also not much been done in terms of training yet. So I read the manuals and came across circulars on the intranet on changes in personnel and other things. Little by little, while getting to know the state of things, a feeling of uneasiness increased and yesterday and today I have shed some tears. At the beginning I have to set my own targets, but in this situation what targets shall I set myself? Also, will I have to content myself with evaluations that are beyond hope? ...Therefore, there is the necessity to think harder about the best method to receive a good evaluation in the easiest way. I won't just say pretty things anymore, flattering men or asking girls how they are; it will all be for myself. Other people have realized this from the beginning and have been doing this for a long time. Since things have changed to the results-based system, it is meaningless to go backwards...Anyway, I wish they would stop unreasonable evaluations.[53]

Finally, there are writers who voice their appreciation of performance-oriented principles, but call for moderation in the way new remuneration systems are introduced. The first writer points out that having stayed with one company for a long time is not necessarily something accidental and companies should come to recognize long service as an ability and achievement. He points to the sense of safety and stability that the existence of older workers provides, but still acknowledges the need of his company to control labor costs by constantly replacing older workers with younger ones.

16 November 2004 – Merit-oriented principle...In the first place, seniority is not a fluke but a capability. No matter what working abilities someone possesses, a person who suddenly quits is troublesome instead of being useful, just troublesome, isn't this true of most workplaces? Employees who can be thought of as trustworthy in terms of their ability to fight for long years are definitely more valuable than employees who may be able to do this and that but may quit next year, in half a year or tomorrow. To completely miss this point and to switch over to the results-oriented pay system is not a good move. In reality, in the case of our puny company, for the first two years after joining the company the basic salary is raised by 10,000 yen. After that, a wage structure has been introduced where during the time of the year when bonuses are paid, the basic wage will be reviewed. As a result, most employees will quit after around 3 years. If the salary is not rising, the motivation to stay on decreases very much ... I have experienced this myself. In the case of my company, they cannot spend more on employees, so every year they successfully recruit new staff from vocational schools or elsewhere. Whether it is someone who is with the company in his second year or someone who has been around for ten years does not matter in terms of his contribution, and one needs to strike a balance. However, if someone has really stayed around for 7 years, it really helps when one thinks in terms of the contributions of that person to a feeling of safety.[54]

This call for balance in the introduction of the new principles is reiterated by another worker.

11 November 2004 – Are you rising? "To be in a seniority-based company where a position of power comes around only after passing the age of 50 means that one has spent 15 hellish years (15 years of solemnly putting up with things)." That's right, I have been putting up with it too! If it is 15 years in hell, I, who have been in the organization for as long as 30 odd years might have transcended into a god by now. Only, things are a bit different nowadays since my company has recently done away with the seniority-based system. In our company there are plenty of middle-aged and young employees who perform well. (Not you, you belong to the elderly group, don't you?) I think it is a very good thing that the seniority-based system has been eroded but things should not become unreasonable. I frankly think that it is a good thing to promote those who perform well, but you surely know that there can be negative aspects when personnel departments don't understand things and this can end up bringing down motivation.[55]

The above writer calls for moderation and care in the application of the new system, and indeed for many employees it seemed to have been less the introduction of merit-based principles as such but rather the ways that new principles were implemented that nurtured anxieties. Blog writers raise a number of issues and these concern issues of transparency as well as the relationship between those who evaluate and those who are being evaluated.

> *8 August 2004 – In today's meeting, there was an announcement from the union that from next year onwards performance-based assessment will be introduced. Well, with salary payout based on the seniority-based system, both capable and incapable people get the same amount, so one can say that this is more appropriate, but ... "Who will be assessing whom?" Well, I hope for an assessment that everyone can understand. This is probably wishing for too much.*[56]

While not being a regular employee, the writer of the next diary entry was still asked to participate in evaluating colleagues. Having had to evaluate her superior she reported that she would have liked to be frank in her evaluation but since she was concerned about anonymity she refrained from voicing her true opinions fully.

> *27 January 2004 – In the company, where I am employed as a dispatch worker, there is a system by which superiors above a certain rank are judged by their subordinates concerning their leadership. Whether they have fulfilled their function as a leader is broken down into categories that are anonymously rated using points and by comments. It is a duty to submit this evaluation. Concerning anonymity, because there are only a few people, I wrote in a brief style, "in a way that is difficult to identify," but I would have liked to have written in more detail, really "harsh things" about my superiors.*[57]

The next diary writer talks about a superior who he felt had acted arbitrarily. Consequently, the writer expressed his satisfaction of having moved to a company where he had more say in the evaluation process.

> *22 June 2004 – Our company is following the trend of the times and has implemented a salary system based on results. My former company also had a results-oriented system, but the superior decided arbitrarily. In the present company, to a certain degree things are decided*

by one's superiors, but one has to work out the details by oneself. There's still hope.[58]

But even if employees have a say in formulating objectives and participating in the evaluation process the question remains of what is the best way to do so.

> *5 April 2004 – Fighting with the results-oriented system – Now I have to write something that matches the scope of the title. I think that currently all companies, together with implementing results/ability-oriented principles, are carrying out management by objectives on a half yearly or yearly basis, and our company is also doing so. In order to administrate these objectives, everyone has to put them together and some people are weak at that. People who are not able to make their work results and skills look appealing end up being underestimated in terms of their results, and if this happens promotion and salary raises are jeopardized ...*

> *Concerning self-evaluation within the actual management by objectives system, one should put oneself one point higher than one really sees oneself and make an effort to stress all the appealing points and results. If one does not highly evaluate oneself, the superior will give an even lower evaluation, and one will therefore not receive a good evaluation. As the superior will not necessarily know one's work content so well, one should also mention things that look good.[59]*

The issues of how to set objectives and what should be the focus of one's evaluation seem to be especially problematic in the context of Japanese workplaces, where work content is often not clearly defined and where most employees are employed as generalists, with companies reserving the right to shift them from one job to another.

> *2 December 2003 – Today's news reported that the largest of Japan's representative manufacturers, the S company, is implementing a "Total Results-oriented Salary Structure." I'm strongly against this ... The reason is that when entering a company "it is impossible to be given only work that one likes and is good at." If one is assigned and diverted to work that one hates and is not good at, having to set one's goals is troubling, as is being evaluated according to how far these goals have been fulfilled ...[60]*

Another writer agrees and adds that working under a results-oriented system takes some of the creativity and joy out of his work, peppering his remarks with some cynical comments about people who prefer the new reward system.

> *4 September 2003 – In this regard, we are currently in the process of preparing the materials and interviews for the half yearly performance appraisals. It cannot be helped. But, I am trapped since the content of my project is special and there is really no work that can be done according to the format. If one just carefully decides to take on many minor tasks, following the details that are specified in the evaluation format, the appraisal will certainly be high. Ah, enough ...*

> *People full of the results-based system are people who take what they have said during the entrance interview for real, who talk about the global level etc. All people like this, please work hard and provide for me by reviving the Japanese economy.*[61]

The following employee reiterates the doubts of previous writers about the possibility of judging achievements fairly and arrives at the conclusion that the introduction of results-oriented systems is largely a disguised cost-cutting measure.

> *13 May 2003 – What to say about results-based remuneration? The news reported that Takeda Pharmaceuticals Company is implementing results-oriented remuneration and boldly reforming the salary system that has been in place until now. It seems that they will change the present seniority-based salary system to one based on ability. What I think every time I see this kind of news is how does one judge employees' ability and results? For example, a pro baseball player's ability clearly manifests itself in figures, and a writer's ability is clearly shown by the number of copies printed. In other words, for most professions, one's productivity is clearly manifested in figures and one gets money according to this. Companies are the same. The company's ability is clearly seen in the figures of profits and sales. However, isn't it impossible to judge each employee's ability in the company in the form of figures? For example, how does one concretely express the results of management staff and product development staff in figures? In the end, companies simply wish to cut labor costs and instead of implementing a measure*

that is incomprehensible, why not just impose an easy to understand salary cut of 15% for all staff?[62]

The final perception concerning the introduction of results-oriented systems comes from a diary writer who doubts whether new evaluation standards were really applied in his company.

15 June 2004 – Today, the section chief announced bonuses and evaluation results. The bonus has risen a little and I received "good" for results. (The real terms used are different but to simplify things, there are four ranks: "very good" "good" "average" and "bad"). Anyway, most people received "average," about 70%. Then 20% got "good" and around 5% either "very good" or "bad." "I did it!" Initially I could not help feeling happy, but this time it is not because I worked hard that my results were good. The process works in this order. University and graduate school graduates are generally promoted; next in line are high school graduates. The results-based system is all lies. This period, I did not work hard at all. If results count, compared to earlier on I have not improved at all, to the point of laughter. After all, my company is like this. No, there are also departments in the company that work hard, so better just say that this is how it is in my department. So even if I don't work hard, next year I will still be promoted (laugh)...makes one want to laugh.[63]

The introduction of results-oriented principles of remuneration has caught the attention of researchers, policy makers and the public, resulting in a number of surveys to find out more about the various issues surrounding this phenomenon. As in the previous chapter, survey results largely support the notions voiced by diary writers, but also add some new points or provided some qualification.

Two relatively simple surveys were conducted via the Internet by Nikkeipb.jp, a sophisticated web portal for information on technology and business run by the leading business publisher Nihon Keizai Shinbunsha. The portal site surveyed visitors and members of its email list twice in regard to the introduction of results-oriented principles, once in June 2004 and again in November of the same year.

Both surveys collected answers from about 2500 participants (mainly male and relatively evenly distributed over age groups) and survey findings pointed to the importance that results-based principles assumed in Japanese corporations, with about 70% of respondents reporting that such principles came to play a large role in their remuneration and advancement. Asked for the effects of results-oriented principles only 23.5% of respondents answered that their workplace perform-ance had improved after the introduction of performance based prin-ciples with the majority admitting to only small or even no effects. Survey participants at the same time reported a number of problems that they experienced with results-based remuneration systems. Issues raised were clarity of standards of evaluation and fairness of evalu-ation with a slight majority of respondents pointing to the existence of problems in both areas. Further 36.7% reported that the introduction of merit principles had worsened the workplace atmosphere and 17.1% reported an increase in the abuse of power by superiors. Yet, it also needs to be stated that 35.2% reported no real influences and 22% saw an improved spirit in their workplaces (Nikkeipb.jp 2004b). Finally, some employees reported more serious consequences of the introduc-tion of merit-oriented principles. 12% answered that the introduction led to depression of some sort for themselves, and 29.6% answered that they knew of people who had experienced depression of some sort. Respondents held various factors responsible for this situation, with the most important ones being discrepancies between wished for work and assigned work, as well as negative effects on personal relationships (Nikkeipb.jp 2004a).

The Institute of Labor Administration (Rōmu Gyōsei Kenkyūjo) (www.rosei.or.jp) surveyed human resources managers and union officials of companies listed on the first section of the Tokyo Stock Exchange in December 2004 and January 2005. The survey results supported previous findings by showing that about two thirds of companies had introduced merit-based systems, with union repre-sentatives giving slightly lower figures (65.6%) than human resources managers (70.1%). Larger companies with more than 1,000 employ-ees were more active in changing remuneration systems than smaller companies (managers: large 77.3%, small 64.2%, union representa-tives: large 69.4%, small 56.8%). Results were not conclusive across all issues addressed but showed that human resources managers saw an increased drive among employees, an overall desire to increase compe-tence and also a general inclination of employees to strive for results. Union representatives confirmed a heightened interest in increasing skills and a stronger orientation towards results, but also pointed to problems such as employees having lost some of the latitude that previously existed in their workplaces (RGS 2005) (Table 4.1).

Opinions were split on the overall functioning of systems. While managers overall assessed their systems as functioning, union officials were more critical (Table 4.2).

88.2% of managers and 93.9% of union representatives reported problems with results-based systems. Asked for specific problems, management and union representatives mainly pointed to issues that were also raised in the blog entries such as the setting, evaluation and management of objectives, followed by employee motivation and development, as well as problems in rotating staff (Table 4.3) (RGS 2005).

Table 4.1 Effects of introduction of results-oriented principles in workplaces in %

| Area | Views by | Affirmative | | | Negative | |
		up	rather up	Neither/ nor	rather down	down
Drive/motivation	management	4.4	57.4	36.8	1.5	–
	union	–	27.5	68.8	3.8	–
Fostering of subordinates	management	–	17.6	69.1	11.8	–
	union	1.3	8.8	68.8	20.0	1.3
Will to increase competence	management	5.9	61.8	32.4	–	–
	union	3.8	45.0	50.0	1.3	–
Results-oriented mood	management	10.3	60.3	25.0	1.5	1.5
	union	2.5	35.0	57.5	5.0	–
Consciousness of competition with colleagues	management	4.4	35.3	58.8	–	–
	union	1.3	38.8	60.0	–	–
Collaboration in groups	management	1.5	11.8	69.1	16.2	–
	union	1.3	3.8	70.0	20.0	5.0
Feeling able to voice own views	management	4.4	20.6	67.6	4.4	1.5
	union	2.5	10.0	68.8	15.0	3.8
Latitude in regard to work	management	–	1.5	69.1	20.6	5.9
	union	–	2.5	36.3	42.5	18.8

Note: Survey of 1,487 human resources managers (response 97) and 886 union representatives (response 122) of corporations listed on the first section of the Tokyo Stock Exchange.

Source: RGS 2005.

Table 4.2   Overall evaluation of performance-oriented systems (in %)

Systems are	Management	Union
functioning	14.7	0.0
functioning quite well	55.9	41.3
neither nor	22.0	42.5
not functioning well	5.9	13.8
not functioning	1.5	2.5

Note: Survey of 1,487 human resources managers (response 97) and 886 union representatives (response 122) of corporations listed on the first section of the Tokyo Stock Exchange.

Source: RGS 2005.

Table 4.3   Problems concerning results-based systems (multiple answers in %)

Problems concerning	Management	Union representatives
Salary and bonuses	28.3	30.7
Evaluation and objectives	93.3	94.7
Ranking and qualifications	28.3	24.0
Development and rotation	31.7	42.7
Pensions and retirement allowances	10.0	8.0
Working hours	15.0	24.0
Motivation	46.7	54.7
Others	–	2.7

Source: RGS 2005.

Another detailed study was conducted by the Japan Management Association. The study found that it would take organizations 4 to 5 years until performance-based remuneration systems bore results (2005a and 2005b). Human resources managers' perceptions of the current workings of their systems were contrasted with their wishes in regard to future development. Thus it became apparent that rather than going back to previous ways, companies were determined to further strengthen the application of merit-based principles. For example, managers were well aware of the fact that not every employee was being utilized in the best possible way yet, but showed a strong desire to rectify this situation. Managers also demanded far more rigor in applying systems, for example by introducing the possibility of demoting employees if performance was not up to expectations (JMA 2005).

Genda and Rebick argued in 2000 that one should see the development towards performance-based evaluation and remuneration as a gradual evolution over time, resulting in flatter earning profiles and larger variations in individual earnings. Similarly, Shibata (2000) (see also Watanabe 2000), by taking up the case of one company in detail, showed that wage differentials existed before the publicly announced introduction of the new systems, with the studied company having introduced performance based elements as early as 1987. However, he then makes what is perhaps a more important point, by arguing that employees were not aware and thereby did not complain about differences since these differences were not made public by employees or unions.

Matanle (2003) also argues that competition did exist in the previous system, however, it was somewhat concealed since employers and employees made efforts to arrange this competition in such ways that it did not become disruptive to personal relationships.

Based on the arguments above, the intensive discussion in Japan concerning developments in wage systems and changing principles of employment can also be interpreted as a matter of heightened perceptions. From a macro-perspective, change might have been of an evolutionary rather than a revolutionary nature. Real effects on intra-firm wage disparities are still difficult to measure and might eventually turn out to be less dramatic than initially expected (Morishima 2002). However, this time round, companies introduced their new systems with great fanfare in the press, wanting to showcase management' resolve, aiming to please investors or to attract the attention of highly motivated and capable employees. Thus, far more than before, these issues became a matter of public discourse and consequentially more people became aware of the existence of income differentials. In addition, large numbers of employees of prominent corporations, often not fully comprehending the new systems as Matsushige 2007 and also the blog entries have shown, were exposed to the effects of the system in their daily lives, not necessarily through changes in their income but through the often troublesome need to set their own objectives and the compulsory participation in regular evaluation exercises.

The public discourse (see also Tatsumichi and Morishima 2007) that developed in Japan surrounding the real or perceived switch to merit-based principles would justify a study of its own and will only be taken up here through the introduction of three popular books, all published during the year 2004. The first book was published in July 2004 by a former employee of Fujitsu's personnel department, Shigeyuki Joe, under the title *The Downfall of the Performance-based Pay System at Fujitsu as Seen by an Insider.* Allegedly, this quickly sold more than 200,000 copies. Fujitsu was a forerunner in the introduction of performance-based wage systems, introducing performance-based annual wages for its managerial staff in 1993 and extending those principles to all its employees in 1998. Subsequently, Fujitsu encountered a number of problems of a nature considered grave enough to endanger the company's competitiveness. Such concerns were not only taken up in the popular press but even the reputable *Nihon Keizai Shinbun* commented that "Fujitsu employees have come to be more concerned about their wage gaps with colleagues than about competition with rival IBM Corp." (NKS-NNI 26 February 2004). Since Joe wrote his book for a mass audience it is difficult to assess the real extent of the problems that occurred within Fujitsu; nevertheless, the book clearly outlines the potential problems of merit-based systems. Among the problems he alleges occurred in Fujitsu are the following (mostly concurring with those already outlined in the blog entries and surveys).

- A drop in morale because employees were grouped into performance bands of pre-determined size, so that many employees who believed that they had fulfilled their own objectives could not be ranked accordingly and were downgraded to lower performance bands.
- Splits in the work force and drops in product quality through the setting of contradictory objectives, for example concerning cost and quality control.
- A tendency of employees to focus only on tasks that were part of their objectives, ignoring irregular but nonetheless important tasks that were not explicitly specified.
- A lack of attention given to strategic tasks; strategic tasks being difficult to quantify and therefore people tending to set themselves achievable tasks of an operative nature.

- Increase of unpaid overtime because of results-based evaluation and remuneration systems.
- An increase in personal costs and inflation of positive evaluations after initial limitations concerning the ranking of employees into bands were eased.

Despite these problems, Joe does not demand a return to the seniority-based system, recognizing that this system was only operational as long as organizations grew continuously. Instead he demands the introduction of performance-based systems that are not simply copies of American systems but are tailored to the Japanese context. He also points out that even American organizations had to adapt their performance-based systems, strengthening the importance of process and long-term-oriented elements, for example by involving customers in evaluation processes.

Another prominent author, University of Tokyo professor Nobuo Takahashi with his book *"Fallacious Performance Principles"* (2004), strongly demanded a return to seniority principles. Takahashi first traces the development of seniority-based pay systems in Japan. He argues that, overall, the concept of a living wage, which was later refined through the addition of a skill-grading system, has served Japanese industries well. The 1990s were not the first time that a change to a more merit-based system was proposed; actually he traces the first proposals back to the late 1960s and then again to the 1980s, with proposals for change always coming up during times of wide-spread corporate crisis. He then repeats the various problems of performance-based pay systems, but draws attention to the fact that many of these systems were introduced by consultants without considering the actual situation within individual companies.

Further, he argues that Japanese companies in fact did introduce performance elements into their advancement and pay systems, but that success did not necessarily result in higher pay or rank. *"While people might be called by the same title 'kakarichō' (assistant manager/sub-section head) the differences between an elite assistant manager and a non-elite assistant manager are clear. Rank and pay might be the same but the actual work content is entirely different."* He sees this subtle differentiation, rewarding people for achievements through job content and remuneration systems providing people with security in life, as constituting a "Japanese style seniority system." This leads to his main argument against the introduction of performance-based systems: higher pay and titles are not the only way to motivate employees; the actual quality of work is more important.

He also counters the argument that the seniority model is only sustainable for growing companies by first pointing out that there are still many growing companies in Japan, and even that for companies that are not growing it should be possible to temporarily restrict annual pay increases. Recognizing flaws in the previous application of the seniority system in Japanese corporations, he suggests a stronger responsibility on the part of superiors to guide their subordinates in skill development.

Takahashi is not the first to bring up the notion of younger workers being rewarded by their work content. For example Itami (1994: 85) argued earlier:

> The best firms certainly do not allow the distribution of status, salary, authority and information to be determined solely by nenko [seniority]; that would soon lower the quality and efficiency of decision making and lead to failure in market competition. Nor, on the other hand, do they allow that distribution to be determined solely by the criterion of ability; that would bring the danger of disruption to social harmony and failure to function efficiently as a group. Hence with non-coinciding distributions, young people are rewarded by the quality of their work content, older people by status and salary. Here again, the essential point is the generation of a sense of fairness; everybody has his own flower, nobody monopolizes the bouquet.

The third book "*The Performance-based Pay System Next Door*" by journalist Norifumi Mizoue refers to the two books discussed above. Mizoue (2004) believes the two books and the subsequent loud echo in the media were responsible for creating a mood swing among employees concerning performance-based principles. He reports that some companies that had been popular with fresh graduates exactly because they had introduced merit principles saw their numbers of applications falling. He also reports that some companies stopped using the term *seika shugi* (result principle) and instead came up with alternative terms such as *jitsuryoku shugi* (ability principle). Overall, Mizoue argues that despite all

the criticism, merit-based pay systems are there to stay and thus
employees need to learn how to deal with them.

Finally, the discussion about merit-based principles needs to be sit-
uated within the larger ongoing domestic discourse about the future
direction of the development of Japanese society. Here the abolishment of seniority and the shift to merit-based principles is being
seen as one of the main underlying factors causing Japan to develop
into what is being called a society of differences (*kakusa shakai*), with
a polarization in terms of economic affluence and societal status. For
example, the national broadcaster NHK brought up merit principles
as one of the key issues leading to a differentiated society in a much
publicized live forum on April 2, 2005, and a newly formed government advisory committee was set up to investigate employment
practices by Japanese corporations in its study about the effects of
large structural change on Japan's economic society (*Sankei Shinbun*
24 March 2005, *Mainichi Shinbun* 13 April 2005). While in reality,
pronounced differences in Japanese society in terms of income have
always existed (Sugimoto 2003), surveys still showed that a large
number of Japanese people (around 90%) believed themselves to
belong to the middle class. The situation in workplaces with a stress
on equality had largely contributed to this self-assessment and such
changes in the management of human resources and an increasing
awareness of their potential consequences can have grave consequences on how people locate themselves within society.

4.3   Drawing consequences: new mindsets, skills and changing jobs

Many employees go further than just describing changes in their
workplaces. They also reflect on how they will have to change their
ways of thinking in a situation where companies are restructuring
and changing principles of work. For the writer of the excerpt below
this starts with a question about what to regard as normal.

> *4 September 2002 – Recession?? What is a recession? To me who has
> never experienced a good economy, the present state is normal. I really do
> not understand how one can rate what elderly and bubble employees talk
> about as being "so very bad at the moment." I myself am optimistic. You
> all must think that I am really naive to say so. Certainly, I also believe that*

currently there is not much work, but regrettably I still cannot understand what is called a good state of the economy and cannot imagine a better situation than now. Rather than falling from the highest place to the lowest, when one only knows the worst state from the beginning, when things improve one can even think a bit, "Oh, isn't the economy doing well?"[64]

Other employees take a more practical stance, arguing that to survive under the new conditions it is necessary to start taking care of one's own future, and an important step in this direction is acquiring abilities and skills that provide some independence.

21 February 2000 – In any company there are many employees that were hired in large numbers during the bubble period. (Actually, I am one of them). These employees have already reached their mid-30s and as employees at a central point in their careers are expected to carry their weight within the company. However, if compared with the small elite of the eras before and after the bubble, they are seen as happy and healthy, but are harshly evaluated for their lack of skills. We, who are like this, have already married, have families and children, have bought apartments with loans, and as such are at the age where we carry the duty of being the central pillar of our families. Currently, when a revival of the economy is not expected, it seems that the target of companies' restructuring has switched from the middle-aged and elderly to the employees who entered during the bubble period. Also, the storm of company bankruptcies has affected big companies without regard for the industry they are in. In addition to that there are frequent mergers on a global scale due to battles for market hegemony.

What is necessary to survive this era of upheaval are "abilities" that can be utilized in the company or in the world, and "a revolution of consciousness" that it is oneself who must look after one's own wellbeing. Presently with human resource policies and salary structures greatly changed to ability/results-oriented pay systems, similar large changes are demanded of salarymen who entered during the bubble.[65]

Another author argues that it might no longer be possible to spend one's whole working life in one company.

18 September 2002 – Now, that the lifelong employment age has come to an end, a trend that sees skills gaining in importance is also gaining ground in Japan. Joining a company and being safe afterwards; that age may have come to an end. In the coming age one will have to distinguish things like, what do I have to do, what is the thing that suits me best, what do I want to do, and one will have to make one's own efforts more and more. Such an era is coming.[66]

Blog writers recognize the necessity to think more about their own future and not only to acquire skills but also be flexible to change.

11 January 2004 – From company standards to global standards – It is of course already gratifying if one is being evaluated by the company, but it is pathetic if one only knows one's own company. If something unexpected should happen and one had to leave, one would be at a loss. Our fathers who galloped through the Showa era [1926–1989] dedicated themselves to just one company under what is called lifelong employment. This is a bit difficult to believe today, but there was an era that regarded this as a virtue. But today, when I think about what is necessary, I think of speed, flexibility, and so on. I will develop myself better based on this view.[67]

Another blog author sees more and more people around him changing employers and after providing a number of examples he relates this to a general change of mindset of employees.

28 October 2000 – Including not only those who have quit to study for further qualifications, but also people who have changed companies, there are many people among my acquaintances who have resigned from their first place of employment. According to statistical data introduced on a program on NHK that I watched earlier, more than 30% of fresh graduates leave their first company within 3 years. Among my acquaintances it is roughly like this: from a certain large publisher (3rd year) to an IT venture company; from a certain large newspaper (3rd year) to studying for the National Bar Examination; from a certain specialist publishing house (2nd year) to another specialist publishing house; from a large city bank (2nd year) to an IT venture company; from a large city bank (2nd year) to a foreign consultancy company; from a large city bank (2nd year) to setting up a private company; from central bureaucracy (2nd year) to specialist foreign trading company; from large city bank (1st year) to pharmaceutical company; from city

*administrator (1st year) to returning to home town; from a certain cos-
metics company (1st year) to freelancer. Our generation began searching
for their first jobs when it had become clear that the long-term employment system had broken down under the influence of the collapse of the
bubble economy. When taking a job there has truly been a change of
mindset, with things having been done away with like "Serving one's
whole life in this company" or "dying for a company."*[68]

Neumark (2000) states that it is quite difficult to verify perceptions
and wishes in regard to job security, mobility, or job stability through
quantitative analysis, and this also applies to Japan. Surveys show that
diary writers are right in their perception that more people are changing jobs; however the question is whether this is really a new phenomenon. It also needs to be noted that it has largely been younger
employees who have changed jobs and that many of them still do so
only once in their careers (Genda and Rebick 2000: Chart 4.2).

A look at other statistics shows an increase in the number of people
who have actually changed jobs, but the situation does not seem to
be as dramatic as perceived by some blog writers (Chart 4.3). What
clearly has increased significantly though is the desire to change

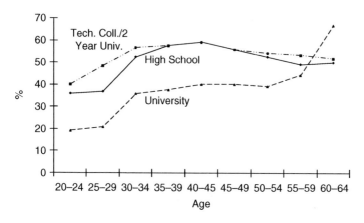

Chart 4.2 Experience of having changed workplaces by educational
qualification in %

Note: Based on official government survey of 440,000 households, October 2002.

Source: Somuchō Tōkeikyoku 2003.

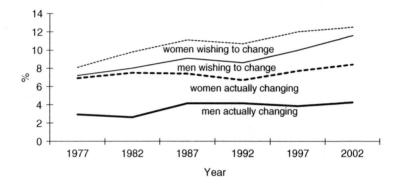

Chart 4.3 Rates of people changing jobs and people wishing to change jobs
Source: based on Sōmuchō Tōkeikyoku 2003.

workplaces. With many women not working as regular employees and not being provided with the benefits that come with this status it is also not surprising that the percentage of women who want to change jobs is higher than that of men.

The relatively low propensity of employees to change employers may be related to a number of factors. First, as already discussed, it is difficult for Japanese employers to selectively dismiss employees. This not only keeps down the number of people who have to look for new jobs involuntarily, but also leads to a lower number of people changing jobs proactively. Another factor inhibiting people from changing companies is the shared investment of employers and employees in firm-specific knowledge and skills, developed by employees through training systems that stress in-house and on-the-job training. Finally, the nature of pension systems also plays a part, with company pensions often being paid out as a lump sum at the time of retirement. Employees voice concerns that claims they have built up over time in terms of seniority wages, pensions or retirement allowances will not be recognized by new employers (Rengo Soken 1994, for a more detailed summary of factors see Genda and Rebick 2000).

This situation reflects underdeveloped external labor markets. Employers and employees alike are uncertain about the supply and demand of labor and the value of qualifications and skills, and this situation increases the necessary time and costs of finding

new employment or new employees. Survey results largely reiterate perceptions of blog writers by showing a high level of uncertainty among employees concerning the value of their own skills.
Other problems encountered by people who have changed jobs were
a lack of information about the situation outside their own company as well as the inability of people to positively sell themselves
to new employers. For example, in a survey commissioned by Japan's
Ministry of Health, Labor and Welfare among 6,300 employees who
were employed mid-career 41% of respondents answered that they
had experienced difficulties understanding the value of their own
skills outside of the company, with 27.8% of respondents citing this
as the greatest difficulty. Other problems included the lack of information about the kind of work (28.9%), the work situation (28.7%) at
other companies or uncertainties about how to appear attractive to
potential employers (20.7%) (Shozugawa 2000, MHLW 2000).

Indeed, Genda (2001) refers to the popular anecdote that was
brought up by one of the blog authors earlier regarding an older
employee who was not able to detail his skills.

> *In fact there is a strong element of truth in the joke: some people whose
> title is 'section chief' have nothing else to recommend them. Quite a few
> other 'section chiefs' have done excellent work and have undoubted abil-
> ity, but simply cannot express themselves in a convincing way to new
> firms and communities. This is because detailed information on how one
> works and the kind of jobs that one has done is available within the firm
> that one belongs to, but one has neither openly talked about such things
> outside the firm nor been asked about them. The punch line 'section
> chief' in the joke is the tragic result of such a climate. Nowadays, people
> are required to be able to explain their own specialties, with some pride
> and dignity, to other people, whether for the purpose of getting a new job,
> or simply within their own firms.*

However, it is not only employees who have problems with the transparency of labor markets. Many companies share similar problems,
admitting to a lack in information on market wages. They also regard
the hiring of employees mid-career as too time and resource con-
suming. In a survey among 2,100 companies conducted in December
1999 over 60% of responding companies reported the costs and time
involved in hiring mid-career employees to be a problem, followed

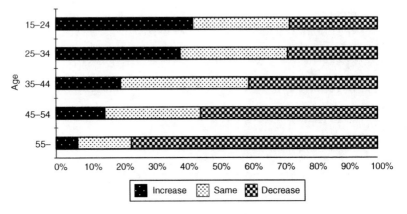

Chart 4.4 Salary change after changing jobs 2004
Note: Labor Force Survey.
Source: Based on Sōmuchō Tōkeikyoku 2005.

by difficulties to establish the market wage (45%) and a lack of intermediaries to help in the search for personnel (35.7%) (Shozugawa
2000, MHLW 2000, Chart 4.4).

The previous chapters have already introduced the argument by
Capelli (1999) who stated that changes in employer-employee relationships only became visible in the US once the economy had picked
up and employees found that their services were in higher demand
again. Indeed, the Japanese economic climate throughout the 1990s
and beyond did not encourage Japanese employees to take risks or
to take the trouble to seek new employment. In staying with their
companies, employees also complied with the expectations of their
employers. While Japanese employers largely want to move to performance-oriented principles they have still voiced their determination to sustain long-term relationships with the members of their
core employee group. In 1995 Nikkeiren (The Japanese Association
of Employers' Associations, merged in May 2002 with the Japan
Federation of Economic Organizations to Nippon Keidanren) published its influential report *"Japanese Management for a New Era"* in
which it proposed a concept that many see as the foundation of
corporate activities today. The report proposed the segmentation of
labor forces into three groups: a core group of regular employees who

are employed long-term but remunerated and promoted based on performance, a group of highly skilled specialists that is employed as long as necessary on a contract basis, and finally employees on the periphery with short-term contracts. The authors of the report believe this approach not only reflects the needs of employers but also the wishes of employees, who are demanding greater choice in terms of employment options (Nikkeiren 1995, Grønning 1998, Kuroda 2006).

Watanabe links the need for the continued importance of long-term employment to strengths of Japanese companies in terms of flexibility and cooperation in workplaces. He sees flexibility and the ability to collaborate in work groups as indispensable traits of the Japanese employment system. He states:

> *The difference is that today Japanese firms have their own production model, whereas in the earlier period they were desperately trying to absorb Western production systems and techniques. There seems to be no reason why they should abandon this model, although it will certainly continue to evolve as it accommodates changes in the market and in technological conditions. If this is the case, it is almost senseless to argue that the employment and wage systems supporting that model will disappear, for that would mean renunciation of the very sources of Japanese firms' competitive strength... This implies that the LES [life time employment system] will probably emerge from the current rationalization movement more or less intact either in factories or in offices, as far as the regular employees of larger companies are concerned.* (Watanabe 2000: 328–329)

However, it has been shown that the close relationship between employees and employers, as well as the existence of lifelong employment with the propensity of employees not to change their corporations, was grounded in a number of push and pull factors, and some of the developments outlined above directly relate to these.

First, as discussed in the previous chapter, there are signs that experiences with downsizing and reorganization have affected the trust of employees in their corporations. This might not have resulted in people leaving companies immediately, but employees might well remember such experiences once more employment opportunities become available again. The same might also be true in terms of the many negative experiences that employees have had when companies started to introduce performance-based employment principles.

However, the introduction of performance-based reward systems might have even more far reaching consequences by raising the employability of people. Having to set their own objectives, evaluating themselves, being evaluated, receiving feedback, and feeling consequences in monetary terms, employees become more aware of their own capabilities and value to the company. Thus, employees who in the past had problems defining and expressing their own strengths and weaknesses are trained to do so through the mechanisms of performance-based pay systems, and they might use this newly acquired capability when offering their skills to other companies.

With more and more companies filling positions through internal advertising and application processes, shifting career responsibility from employer to employee, employees are gaining further skills in marketing themselves. While overall only 31.2% of companies have so far introduced the procedure of advertising available positions in-house, this is clearly a trend within larger corporations, reaching over 80% for corporations with more than 5,000 employees (regular survey by Japan Productivity Organization, Nov/Dec 2004, 2,722 companies, response 253) (JPCSED 2005a). The same survey also showed that a number of companies are in the process of introducing differentiated wage systems based on occupation. Results showed that 15.9% of companies had already introduced or were set to introduce such a change, while another 32.4% were studying the introduction. Nevertheless, 50.2% of corporations answered that they were currently not planning to follow this path, with most companies stating that this would lead to difficulties in regard to the rotation of employees between occupations and tasks, as well as pointing to the non-existence of well-defined and recognized occupational profiles in Japan. Companies were also afraid of consequences in regard to the morale of employees who would end up being employed in low salary occupational groups (JPCSED 2005a).

Another development that changes the relationship between employers and employees is changes in regard to welfare benefits and pensions. A survey conducted on employment practices in Japan by the Japan Productivity Center for Socio Economic Development (JPCSED 2004a) (2,626 listed companies, 9.7% response rate) found that while 82.5% of corporations were paying a family allowance, 25.9% of companies planned to abolish or reduce this practice. A housing allowance was paid by 66.9% of firms but 21.5% of companies planned to abolish this practice totally or to cut benefits. While Chapter 2 has shown examples of companies that have largely abandoned corporate pensions and retirement allowances, other companies, with strong support and encouragement from the government, are introducing pension plans with portability of benefits, which makes it easier for their employees to switch companies (Usuki 2002).

Employees have also become more interested in acquiring qualifications on their own and developing their careers independently. In the large survey of employee perceptions in regard to work that was carried out by the Japanese Institute of Labor Policy and Training (JILPT 2004b) 54.1% of respondents stated that skill development had definitely become more important over the last three years, and another 33.4% answered that this activity had become rather more important. Not surprisingly, it was especially employees in their forties who recognized this fact, with 52% of employees of this age group stating that skill development had become more important. Employees are increasingly choosing companies for the opportunities they offer in developing skills and careers, while the future of the company itself has lost in importance. A regularly conducted survey by the Japan Productivity Center for Socio Economic Development among newly employed young people found that while in 1971 among a variety of motivations the future prospects of the company had been the most important reason for employees to choose their company (27%) this figure has dropped by the year 2004 and the possibility to develop own skills and personality has become the most important reason (32%) followed by the level of interest of work that the new job promises (23.5%) (JPCSED 2004b). At the same time, relationships outside the company have become more important for employees, supporting the notion of a reduced importance of companies to their employees (Shozugawa 2000). However, this does not mean that work itself has lost in importance. The survey by the Japan Productivity Center also asked newly hired young employees for their priorities between work and life. While the majority of newly hired employees responded that they wanted to balance life and work (80%), the proportion of those workers who prioritized quality of life over work declined from 23%

in 1991 to 10% in 2004 (JPCSED 2004b). It was probably easier to take a stance of prioritizing quality of life in a period where work opportunities were abundant and everyone was assuming that Japan was on its way towards a leisure society. The authors from the Japan Productivity Center interpreted their survey results as portraying a shift from starting a career at a certain company to starting work in general (JPCSED 2004b). Matanle (2003: 135), based on available survey data as well as his own fieldwork, agrees with this assessment, stating,

> *Nevertheless, although we must caution against understanding present developments as a mirror of Anglo-American modern individualism, there is a steadily though gradually growing desire among employees for more fluid careers that may involve working for a number of different employers. This might be interpreted as a move in the direction of Western-style multi-company specialized career chimneys.*

Finally, employees are supported in their quest for greater independence from their companies by initiatives of Japanese policy makers. Japanese policy makers have been studying developments outside Japan and are well aware of the concept of employability as a possible new foundation of stable employer/employee relationships. A report of a study group set up by the Ministry of Health and Welfare presented a report concerning the concept of employability in 2001. The main problem that was pointed out by this group was the lack of widely recognized job categories and qualification standards, and the panel therefore advised policy makers to come up with initiatives in this regard (Kōsei Rōdōshō Kenkyū-kai 2001). The issue of employability has also become an issue for Japanese corporations within the overall growing discussion on corporate social responsibility. While an early report by the relatively progressive Keizai Doyukai (Japan Association of Corporate Executives) still judged employability largely to be the responsibility of employees (Keizai Doyukai 2000), a later survey on the state of corporate social responsibility assigned responsibility to employers, but assessed corporate efforts as still lagging behind (Keizai Doyukai 2004: 2).

The advance of the Internet has also increased the transparency of external labor markets for employees and employers alike. Japanese corporations are actively using the Internet to establish contacts with potential employees, and many companies have a section on their web pages that addresses hiring policies and needs, not only for fresh graduates but also in terms of mid-career hiring. For example, Matsushita set up a detailed site at https://fortuna.jcareers.com/matsushita/u/pos.phtml to recruit employees with specialist skills mid-career in such areas as technology, law and accounting. The site encouraged employees by stating that Matsushita hired 300 people mid-career in 2004 and planned to hire 350 such employees in 2005. Yet, although the company hired a total of 1,200 employees during the year 2004, the majority of new employees were fresh high school or university graduates. Nevertheless, this development was seen as a major change in the recruitment policies of large corporations (*Mainichi Shinbun* 19 March 2005). In addition, a number of companies have appeared that attempt to act as intermediaries in linking potential employees and employers and thereby help both sides to deal with the non-transparent nature of the Japanese labor market. Finally, the Internet also allows employees to exchange views with each other; Internet blogs obviously being part of this discourse. While it is usually difficult to discuss issues of changing work with colleagues at one's own workplace, a large number of Internet forums have sprung up that allow employees to anonymously seek advice and exchange experiences in regard to changing companies.

This chapter draws towards its conclusion by presenting a bolder vision of the future development of the management of human resources in Japanese corporations. In the April 2005 issue of its magazine *Works,* Works Institute, the research arm of influential human resources company Recruit Co., publicized its own projection of the future of Japanese human resources management entitled *"Let's cultivate the business professional."* In an interesting approach, Works Institute linked current developments into a larger historical perspective. Like so many other publications it compared the development that began in the 1990s to those of the Meiji Period (1868–1912). The authors of the study argue that the change to performance-oriented principles from the 1990s onwards might, or rather should, just be seen as a transitional stage with the ultimate goal of overcoming the heritage of the previous period. For them the heritage that needs to be overcome is the incentive systems that were set up with the purpose of rewarding the acquisition of skills by production workers and at the same time had the purpose of nurturing generalists who were able to provide leadership in fast-growing pyramid-shaped organizations. Expecting that companies would have to flatten their hierarchies further and overcome the problem of a smaller pool of available personnel due to a generally shrinking population, Works Institute argues for cultivating business professionals who possess high technical and managerial expertise. This would be a return to ability-oriented principles, but on a higher level (Ōkubo 2005). In contrast to the earlier model by Nikkeiren, that saw the Japanese corporation of the future being separated into a relatively small group of core employees with general managerial skills supported by a large number of specialists and irregular employees, in this model the specialized and highly capable professional would assume a role at the centre of the organization. Works Institute proposed this change under the slogan *"From organizational man to professional."* Realizing that this was a drastic change, the researchers of Works Institute demanded changes, from employees as well as corporations, in the education system and in government policies (other articles in *Works*, no. 69, April–May 2005).

This chapter has looked at the employer-employee relationship in a period where employment principles were being challenged. Japanese corporations came up with a number of initiatives to change principles of employment and blog entries have shown that these changes have significantly influenced perceptions of employees concerning their work situation. In particular, the introduction of results-oriented incentive systems, while welcomed by some employees, has been viewed with much apprehension by others and it needs to be seen whether Japanese corporations will be able to come up with solutions to adapt this principle to their employees' and their own satisfaction.

While Japanese corporations would like to separate aspects of seniority and long-term employment this seems to be difficult. Through various mechanisms the introduction of results-oriented principles has led to more transparency in labor markets and thus enables employees to change companies more easily.

The main test of the significance of current developments in employment relationships will only come once the economy improves significantly again or possibly when employers face a shortage of labor due to Japan's low birthrate, as some have predicted.

The question is whether employers in this situation will return to the emphasis on paternalistic values or whether they will succeed in finding ways to combine their own self-interest with the interests of increasingly individualistic employees. However, the next chapter, which deals with the diversification of employment types, will show that for many employees, issues of seniority and lifelong employment have already lost most of their importance either by choice or by economic need.

5
Taking Up Non-Regular Employment

14 March 2003 – There is talk that Y-san from the materials group who originally came with me from the same company, K. Heavy Industries, is going to resign happily soon...After she leaves, I will essentially be the only regular employee left...Nowadays in order to cut costs, they are paying for dispatch workers everywhere.[69]

8 December 2003 – I am going to turn 30 in March. The Japanese recession has deepened, so I honestly don't know what will happen. Honestly, I have many feelings of uncertainty. So I have become determined that I really do not want to fail when changing jobs next time. I feel that companies are employing arubaito [irregular, mostly student workers] and dispatch workers and are reducing the number of regular workers.[70]

Looking at restructuring and changing employment principles, the previous chapters focused mostly on the situation of male employees who were regularly employed at larger Japanese corporations. Indeed, the treatment of such employees has largely shaped the popular understanding of Japanese employment practices. While the number of Japanese employees who enjoyed the privileges and benefits of this kind of employment to the fullest was in fact limited, the underlying principles still constituted strong societal ideals in terms of personal ambitions and life courses. Yet, Japanese companies are changing the composition of their workforces. In 2004 the number of non-regular employees reached 16 million employees, or roughly one third of Japan's working population (Table 2.4). This development not only threatened the position of regular employees but also created new employment realities for a large share of the Japanese workforce.

> *22 December 2003 – Who to work for? Of course, since I came on a contract to do accounting, I will be made to leave if another [regular] accounting person is hired, and they will look for another job for me again. But this is also the reason why one works as a dispatch worker. I think, for a normal company, especially a large company, one enters the company on the assumption that one cannot say anything, no matter what department one is assigned to. But dispatch workers such as me have things they want to do for themselves, and have become dispatch workers so they do not have to do things apart from that. For that reason, one gives up bonuses and bears the risk of not having a retirement allowance and security, just in order to somehow follow one's own intentions.*[71]

The writer of the blog excerpt above works as a dispatch worker, a kind of employment status that is subsumed under the term of non-regular employee in Japan. Non-regular employees are characterized by all or some of the following attributes: not having a regular unlimited contract, being paid by the hour, working shorter hours per day or for a limited period of time and, most importantly, being treated differently by employers in terms of remuneration and welfare benefits. The terminology used in companies differs and is usually not very precise, with some so-called part-timers working as long as regular employees in terms of working hours.

> *27 January 2004 – Since February I have been working as a medical clerk in the position of a full-time part-timer (working somewhere with no regular employees is depressing). I continue my search for a job where I will work as a regular employee, because part-time work carries the image of being a housewife...However, will I be all right without any specialist knowledge or experience...I am terribly frightened of what will happen if I get fired.*[72]

The above statements by blog writers also provide a first insight into the diversity that needs to be dealt with when looking into the issue of non-regular employment, with people working in a variety of employment patterns and for a variety of motives. While it will be shown that in the past, non-regular employment in Japan was relatively clearly compartmentalized in terms of supply, demand and needs of employees and employers, the situation became much more complex from the 1990s onwards with non-regular employment spreading across all socio-demographic groups and all sectors of the economy.

The increase in the number of people working in non-regular employment and the increasing diversity of working patterns quickly became a major topic of public interest, with media, academia and policy makers speculating about the future implications of this trend for Japan's economy and society. Some blog writers use this discussion as a starting point to reflect on the issues, while others simply report their own experiences. Looking at diary entries, issues that are of concern to the authors can be summed up under the following four themes: the motivation to take up non-regular employment, anxieties that come with this kind of work, roles that employees perform in their workplaces, and expectations and anxieties in terms of future career development.

Introduced by an overview of the different types of non-regular employment, this chapter begins by discussing the first two issues, then goes on to give an introduction to the general discussion on non-regular work in Japan. It thereby sets the stage for the following chapter, which will take up the other two issues and will also further locate non-regular employment within the overall development of Japanese labor markets and employment practices.

5.1   Types of non-regular employment

Diary entries show that people take up employment as so-called non-regular employees for a number of reasons and in various employment categories, many of which are difficult to define properly. In one of the diary entries above one writer used the puzzling term "full-time part-timer" to describe her situation, and this is just one indicator of the complexities involved. Indeed, Japanese mainly use the term *paato* (part-timer) not to describe a clearly defined contractual pattern of employment but rather a socio-demographic group (Broadbent 2001). When using the term

"part-timer," they are thus referring to married female employees in their thirties to fifties who gave up work after marriage but
have re-entered the workforce, working shorter hours and often
performing relatively simple tasks that are different from the work
they did before getting married.

On closer inspection, so-called part-timers can be separated into
two groups. The first group consists of women mostly in their forties
and fifties. Their children have already gained independence and
this allows their mothers to work long hours, more than 30 a week,
and quite often close to or even equal to the hours of regular employees; thus the somewhat paradoxical term of "full-time part-timers."
The second group consists of younger women in their thirties who
still have to dedicate much time to their households and therefore
work less than 30 hours (Ribault 1999).

Part-time employment in the above sense is not new to Japan, and
the case of the writer below is rather typical. Having quit her position in administrative work when she got married she could only
re-enter the labor force as a waitress when she decided to start working again.

> *9 April 2003 – Talking about work…Since getting married, I am now
> working for the first time in ten years. Previously, I did desk work. But
> eventually I abandoned the thought of administrative work, since my
> young child is still small and I did not want to have to put up with con-
> straints such as overtime, etc. I could not find a workplace that would
> be good for me…So, I am now working in an outlet of a certain restaur-
> ant chain. I really wanted to work in the kitchen but at the time of the
> interview I dared not answer "no" to the question "Are you prepared to
> work as a waitress?"*
>
> *Less than one month has passed since I began work, and I would like to
> say that overall I have already got quite used to the work. Me and also
> the children…But, really, work is hard. My fullest respect goes to all
> wives grinding their teeth working and at the same time taking care of
> their households. Of course, also to husbands, who work hard to support
> their families.*[73]

While the above writer later managed to somewhat improve her situation by finding work that was more to her liking in a photo print shop,[74]

the below entry shows the thoughts of a younger woman who has just made the decision to quit her position as a regular employee to get married. As with the previous writer, it is especially the long working hours that make it difficult to continue working as a regular employee.

> *13 January 2004 – Watershed 2: I made the big decision to quit working... "Work and marriage" "marriage and Shovel," I have become more and more concerned about various issues and it was worrisome that for a long long time I could not come up with an answer... I want to marry soon☆, but if I marry it will become difficult to save money and if this is so, it will also become difficult to buy the Shovel... Having said that, I also hate to delay marriage. "Work and marriage" ... There is also the idea of continuing to work hard as a regular employee, but when my mate comes home I really want to give him a hot meal and prepare a hot bath, I also really want to take care of my kids and don't want to leave them to other people. So there are various worries that seem to make it difficult to continue being a regular employee.*[75]

The Shovel mentioned in the entry is not a garden tool but a Harley motorcycle, demonstrating that there is more to work motivations than just the popular and often polarized alternatives of family life or career. However, people are influenced in their decisions by restrictions in their environment. The next blog entry is a response by a diary writer after she was asked by a female friend whether she had someone among her acquaintances who could offer her work.

> *3 February 2004 – Having gotten married at 30, it is impossible for her to become a regular employee. One does not know when she will get pregnant and it would be unbearable for the company if half a year after becoming a regular employee she quit, saying "I am pregnant." If one thinks about the risk for the employer, there is no place that would employ her in the first place. The companies where my friends are working can also not afford to take such a risk. In this case it is better to become an arubaito, part-timer, or agency worker. Because the salary is good for dispatch work, I looked around.*[76]

In her response, the above blog writer mentioned two forms of non-regular employment in addition to the already introduced part-time work: *Arubaito* and agency or dispatch work (*haken*). The word *arubaito* from the German word *Arbeit* entered the Japanese language through its usage by high-school and university students to describe their work outside their obligations at school, and is today widely used by employers too. As for *paato* this term is used to describe the type of work as well as the person performing the task.

> *1 November 2004 – Arubaito at night: I have worked as an arubaito at night without interruption since I went back to school. For three years now I have been employed at a contract company that works for a company listed on the first section of the Tokyo Stock Exchange (a drug wholesaler). I work after my classes, so the time is convenient and the hourly wage is 1,000 yen, with a night time allowance of 50% and an overtime allowance of 50%. If I have a good reason, for example because of clinical training, I can take time off.*[77]

While *paato* are restricted by family obligations, *arubaito* usually face restrictions due to their study schedules, and therefore often work at night. In the case of the writer above, his status is further complicated by the fact that he is working for a contractor who has taken over part of the operations of a wholesaler, probably on the premises of the wholesaler itself. As outlined earlier, this is an increasingly common practice in Japan and is a growing source of non-regular employment.

The writer of the next blog entry is employed under similar conditions. Still a student, he wants to develop a career in the dispatch industry and thus regards his employment not only as an opportunity to earn money but also to gain experience.

> *5 February 2005 – Since yesterday I have a new arubaito job. For the first time I am experiencing so-called mass production...The work is quite tiresome. From 9 am in the morning till 5 I am very much imprisoned in the factory. On top of that, it is simple, repetitive work. It came to me that earning a living can be really hard...It was the first time I had worked in a factory like this, with no connection at all with people outside. It really was a new experience...I will be working in the dispatch industry in the future, but this was the so-called on-site contract industry. So I could see the situation of people working as contract workers. While slightly different I think that it is important to gain first-hand experience this way. There are things one does not understand if one has not experienced them in reality, and there are also things one can study.*

*I think I am fortunate to be able to work and study at the same time.
And one also builds bodily strength and muscles.*[78]

The type of so-called non-regular work that has received the most
attention over the last couple of years is temp agency work or dispatch work (*haken*). Here, employees are not employed by the actual
workplace in which they are working, but with an agency that dis-
patches them to clients. Occupations that could be performed under
this status used to be restricted by government regulations, but with
changes to the law the scope of occupations was widened, and in
this process the number of dispatch workers increased rapidly. Most
administrative tasks as well as counter operations in services and
the financial industry became possible fields of employment by dispatch workers, and later even factory work was included in the list
of allowed occupations. Being relatively new and gaining popularity
quickly, dispatch work became a popular topic with blog authors.

The Labor Force Survey provides an overview of the importance
of different types of employment over time. This survey categorizes
employees roughly into regular and non-regular employees. Non-
regular employees are then further divided into part-time employees,
arubaito, dispatch employees, contract or entrusted employees and
other employees. Even the Labor Force Survey thus avoids a stringent
classification, categorizing employees based on the terminology used
in their own workplaces (Table 5.1).

The survey first shows the clear separation of employment types in
Japan along gender lines. Men represent 57% of all employees, but 70%
of regular employees. Women represent 69% of non-regular employees. Most clearly dominated by women is the part-time category, with
90% of employees in this group being women. In comparison the
group of so-called *arubaito* that used to be mostly composed of high-
school and university students working in addition to their studies
has an equal distribution of male and female workers.

While there is a clear dominance of women in dispatch work, men
have a slight majority in the group comprising so-called contract or
entrusted employees, as well as among remaining workers who do not
fall into any of the other groups. Many employees belonging to these
later categories are male retirees who continue to work, either due to a
low mandatory retirement age in their companies or because their company has asked them to switch to a different type of employment.

Table 5.1 Composition of Japanese workforce by employment type 2007 (employees in 1000)

	Total Employees	Regular	Non-regular	Part-time	arubaito	Employed at dispatch company	Contract and entrusted	Other
Total	51740	34410	17320	8220	3420	1330	2980	1370
Female	22340	10390	11940	7390	1700	800	1370	690
Male	29410	24020	5380	830	1720	530	1610	680

Source: Based on Sōmuchō Tōkeikyoku (2008).

5.2   Voluntary or lack of alternatives?

People have a number of reasons for becoming dispatch workers. For the first writer this was simply the only kind of work he was offered after graduation.

> *6 October 2002 – One year. In one week, I will have worked as a company employee (shakaijin) for one year. In my case, I have been a "newly graduated dispatch worker" employed on a one-year contract. After that I'll have to choose whether to try to become a regular employee, to continue to work as a contract employee or to go to another company. As one year will be over soon, what will happen? I asked the dispatch company... "How about extending the contract for four months?" I was told. As for me, I would like to stay in this company for longer and see a bit more, so I accepted the extension. After that I don't know if I will become a regular employee, but I was given a chance called "employment." Well, that's the crucial word. "Grab the chance!"*[79]

The author of the next diary entry became a dispatch worker because it was the closest he could get to his chosen profession, but unfortunately, he realized later that the work of a dispatch worker was not the same as that of a regular employee.

> *13 March 2002 – During my second round of looking for a job I got into the final round of interviews with a large advertising company H, but I failed. Afterwards I studied for the exam to become a certified public accountant, but I still wanted to work in the advertising industry, so I joined company H as a dispatch worker. I worked for half a year, but then I resigned since I felt that there were great differences between the work of a dispatch worker and that of a regular employee. So from now on I will begin again to look for work as a regular employee.*[80]

Another blog author voiced uncertainty about what and where to work, and therefore described dispatch work as a chance to experience different workplaces.

> *25 December 2003 – What's a dispatch worker? Lately, I have become interested in what is called dispatch work. When I quit my last company, a relative who lives in the Tokyo area said "How about registering as a*

dispatch worker and trying a variety of work?" But I insisted that "there aren't any dispatch jobs in the countryside!" But now, even here, there are several big dispatch companies lined up, and I have been thinking that perhaps there will be some work for me here. Somehow, to an inexperienced eye, it feels as if a dispatch worker is the same as a freeter. Is that so? ... Perhaps I should just ask about it. As I am a very inconsistent person, if possible, I would like to use the position of a dispatch worker to try all kinds of jobs. Eventually, I will find something, maybe.[81]

Besides stating his hopes concerning dispatch work, the diary writer also introduces the term *freeter (furiitaa)*, though she is not sure whether this term applies to her. The Kenkyusha dictionary lists the term as a contraction of the words *furii* and *arubaita* (free + the term for student helpers), and says it is used to describe a job-hopping part-time worker, a permanent part-timer or a part-timer by choice. The term *freeter* was initially coined in the late 1980s for people who went against the convention of looking for work as regular employees immediately after they graduated from high school or university and instead took up irregular employment. Since then, the term *freeter* has assumed prominence in an intense discussion about the mindset and situation of young people in Japan.

The following blog author represents the *freeter* generation, showing the attitudes but also the anxieties that people of this group share. The availability of dispatch work provided her with the freedom to pursue her interests during the summer months. Nevertheless, the writer realizes that this lifestyle has its risks, with advancing age threatening employability, even for people who are still only in their twenties.

5 April 2002 – Regrets about this and that: I am turning 28 soon. There are many places that only employ people below thirty for administrative positions. I often think that it would have been better if I had followed a more long-term strategy in job-hunting, looking for a job as a regular employee. However, I had no money ... And it was hard to just sit at home every day. While sitting through the job interviews I had to realize that I had not changed since I gave up work as a regular employee a year ago. I regretted that I had not picked up more solid qualifications, and thought that I should have prepared application materials that made me look more appealing. So, my self-confidence vanished ... "You have already worked three times in short-term dispatch positions"; of course I was asked about this during the interviews. To tell the truth, I wanted to enjoy myself during summer, so I took short-term jobs. If I had said this it would really have become a minus factor, so of course I could not tell the truth – that because I wanted to enjoy myself in summer, I worked only short-term (laugh).[82]

Like the writer above there are many others who stress the various aspects of freedom that non-regular work offers to them.

7 January 2003 – Working in a company, no matter what, one must take associating with other people seriously. The team within the department where I am working has a New Year party, but I feel quite strongly against going. If I refused, will things turn bad? Selfish, isn't it? But look at it this way, among dispatch workers there are people who have chosen this type of work because they don't want to engage in personal relationships.[83]

Another writer argues likewise.

8 May 2001 – Last year, I quit the place where I had worked as a regular employee due to some trouble, and currently I do not feel like working in a regular job. The long working hours are restrictive and personal relationships are annoying. Because hospitals are mainly a workplace for women it is pretty tough ... So far I am still a part-time employee. It may be the right time to look for a full-time job.[84]

The two writers above stress the possibility of distancing themselves from intricate personal relationships, while the writer of the abstract below describes herself as a "happy-go-lucky" dispatch worker and was surprised when she was offered the chance of building a career.

14 January 2004 – The department head cares a lot about me. This man is also on the board of the company, an important person. "Why don't you become a regular employee?" he said. There are several hundred dispatch workers in the company. There seem to have been no cases of female dispatch workers becoming regular employees so far. I was surprised. Less than two months have passed so why does he think "she can do it." "Eventually I want you to become my right-hand person,"

*he said... What? I had no intention of working like that for this com-
pany... I'm just a happy-go-lucky dispatch worker.*[85]

The next two writers reiterate the feeling of being less restricted than
regular employees in their status as dispatch workers. Both writers
want to have a say in the tasks they are assigned.

*16 March 2003 – I am not a robot, I am human. Whatever I do I want
to do it in a manner worthy of myself. For this reason, I also have no
regrets about my current work style (as a dispatch worker). However,
this does not mean that dispatch work simply equals living in a manner
worthy of oneself. The reality is that one has to work hard quite often
(wry smile).*[86]

The second writer adds to this point the inability to cope with corporate hierarchies.

*19 January 2004 – Compared to the boring regular workers (especially
office ladies and such), I think that I can be more useful as a dispatch
worker (however, bonuses, regular pay increases and transport allowance are all no good) and that it suits me better. And please also look at
my character. I am a type who likes to oppose pressures that come from
the top (laugh).*[87]

Finally, there is a group of people who have arrived in so-called non-
regular employment at the initiative of their companies. Employees
keep their workplaces, but do not appear any longer as regular
employees on the official company payroll.

*8 June 2004 – I have concluded a contract with the company. From
next week on I will switch to the position of a "contractor." This is neither an arubaito, nor a regular employee; boldly stated it seems to be
"self-employed" (laugh). The company assigns work to me for a commission, the payment will become my so-called wages; however since
it is contract work it is not wages; it falls into the categories of fees,
remuneration, or charges. Therefore, there will be no health insurance
and no social insurance. I will also have to make a final tax declaration
(sour smile). The woman sitting at the desk next to me is also a former
employee, but it seems that she changed several years ago to this type*

of work. I do not really talk with her, she is several years older than me, but she is single and there is the rumor that she drives a Mark II and a Crown [cars]. In months where there is no work, there is of course no pay, but in months where there is work it seems that one can earn between 600,000 and 800,000 yen, on average more than 300,000 yen per month. U-n, my goal is to earn as much as she does.[88]

While the above writer has just entered into an agreement with her company to become an independent contractor the writer below did so a couple of years previously. However, with his company being absorbed by the parent company he is going to lose his main source of income, while his former colleagues still under regular contracts will keep their jobs.

17 July 2001 – Company folds. I will lose my job…It was announced officially yesterday that the company where currently I am mainly working is folding…To put it simply, it will be absorbed by the parent company. Times are like this. It must be what they call a rationalization measure. So the regular employees are basically moved to the parent company. The problem is the workers under contract…Actually, long ago I came into this company as a regular employee, moreover, as a new employee. However, I was assigned to an unsuitable post and bore it for 4 years…As to be expected, I lost the will to work. Actually, I had intended to wash my hands of this company totally, but I was asked to stay as there was a shortage of personnel. I was able to work freely, and so I remained as a contract worker.[89]

The previous chapters have already addressed the complexities involved in the restructuring moves of Japanese corporations in some detail; employees voluntarily or involuntarily being transferred or retiring early. The following entry summarizes many of these developments and adds further complexity. While the previous chapters have looked mainly at the situation of male employees, this entry also deals with the situation of female employees, some of whom have been pressured to resign or to change their contractual status to non-regular employment.

28 March 2003 – Because my current contract is only till the end of April, the previous month was a period when my destiny was decided (laugh). Anyhow, this round again I have not been fired; I managed to get an extension of my contract for another half year. Hoh! But, since the merger has been decided, it seems that there will be various organizational changes. The department next to ours has been shrunk, and many people have resigned. We dispatch workers don't know the details, but people were recruited for early retirement. There were about 50 single female employees too many, and these people have quickly been made to resign. People are being robbed of their workplace, retiring without knowing what to do. It seems that there was also soft restructuring a few years ago. People belonging to the group of housewives who have worked for many years as regular employees were all made to change to the status of "dispatch" workers. This was done in a vicious way. It is said that there were only two choices for them, either to resign or to become dispatch employees.

And it seems that the young girl that was shifted last year has also resigned. I met her today and greeted her saying, "we have been lonely here since you left us." She said that at the place to which she was transferred there was nothing to do. So I said that this seemed to have been restructuring by "ordering someone to work in the archives [connotation of morgue]." [She answered:] "I have continued to work, but when my work was taken away from me I could not endure another moment. It would be good if I could find other work."[90]

The diary excerpts serve to show and illustrate the existence of a diversity of motives for working in irregular employment patterns but cannot really explain which motives are of higher importance or representative for most people. So, as previously, the accounts and perceptions of diary writers need to be contrasted, complemented and qualified with the help of survey results and statistical materials.

Diary writers have complained about lower wages and they are right in their perception that they are paid less than regular workers doing the same job. The union affiliated Rengo Research Institute for Advancement of Living Standards (Rengo-Rials 2002) analyzed wage structures in a study commissioned by the Ministry of Health, Welfare and Labor. Taking a closer look at the wages for part-time workers it went beyond the usual aggregation where wages are compared regardless of possible differences in work content. The survey first found that the aggregated figures showed an average hourly wage for female regular employees (average age

37.6 years) of 1,350 yen compared to an average hourly wage of only 889 yen for part-time employees (average age 43.6 years). Taking into account other benefits and calculating hourly wages over the span of a year would increase the hourly wage for regular female employees by 349 yen, but by only 53 yen for part-time employees (Rengo-Rials 2002).

The diary entries have shown that for many employees the convenience and choice that non-regular work offers in terms of the location of workplaces and working hours is an important advantage of non-regular work, a perception that is reinforced by survey results (Table 5.2).

Indeed, in the discourse on non-regular work in Japan a major argument is that for many non-regular employees the possibility of combining work with other obligations and interests outweighs higher monetary rewards as well as anxieties concerning job security and social benefits. Thus this argument sees non-regular employment as largely voluntary. Osawa (2001), in an overview of different theoretical explanations for women taking up non-regular work and accepting wage differentials, calls this the "compensation wage hypothesis." University of Tokyo professor Hiroki Sato (2001) supports this view. Based on a number of surveys of work satisfaction, he argues that non-regular workers show high levels of satisfaction and are thus working in the employment type of their choice.

Table 5.2 Ranking of reasons for working in current company (%)

Rank	Regular	Part-time*	Dispatch
1	Job security 36.6	Contributing to household and educational costs 51.6	Short commute 30.2
2	Income security 26.8	Short commute 36.4	Work that matches qualifications 23.5
3	Rewarding work 23.8	Choice of working hours 33.9	No alternative 21.5
4	No alternatives 20.6	Pleasant work environment 18.2	Increase capabilities 19.2
5	Short commute 20.0	Income security 17.4	Contributing to household and educational costs 18.2

Note: Up to three multiple answers, * part-timers working short hours.
Source: JILPT 2004b: 392.

According to Table 5.2, non-monetary rewards are not only important for the group comprising married female part-timers but also for
dispatch employees. Yet, 21.5% of dispatch employees still state the
involuntary nature of their choice of employment type. While Sato
(2001) argues that percentages in the 10s and 20s are of lower significance, this still constitutes a significant number of people in abso-
lute terms, especially with the number of dispatch employees having
more than doubled since the time he wrote his article.

In addition to the "compensation wage hypothesis" Osawa (2001)
discusses a number of other theoretical approaches that have been
brought forward to explain the situation of non-regular employees
in Japan. The first is the "human capital hypothesis," which argues
that companies spend less on the training of non-regular employees
since these normally work shorter hours and stay with the company
for shorter periods. Thus, it is the gap in qualifications that explains
lower wage levels. Another explanation brought forward was the
"efficiency wage theory," which largely attributes the segmentation
of workforces to individual productivity. Here employers pay a premium to regular employees, expecting them to take on higher responsibility and also to make spontaneous efforts when necessary. With
regular employees usually working in teams this premium is seen as
necessary, since individual real effort cannot be measured appropri-
ately. In contrast, individual contributions of part-time workers are
seen as being easily assessable with no special effort expected from
them, so that no premium needs to be paid and pure market productivity wages apply.

Osawa (2001), however, rejects most of these explanations, pointing out that within these models there is no room to explain the
existence of so-called non-regular employees who work as many
hours as regular employees and might do so with the same or even
more skill and energy.

*Those who approve of differences in treatment between regular and
irregular workers must first establish that there is a clear and substantial
difference in the degree to which the two types of workers are constrained
in their activities by their companies. Is the loss of freedom suffered by
regular workers really so much worse than for part-timers that it war-
rants compensation in the form of wages for regular workers that are
30% higher.* (Osawa 2001: 198)

Instead she points to work by Yoshifumi Nakata (1997) and Nobuko Nagase (1995) and Furugōri Tomoko (1997) who argue that lower wages for female employees are simply a direct consequence of gender or the status of being a non-regular employee and should thus be seen as an outcome of discrimination.

Indeed, there are a rising number of non-regular employees whose work content does not differ much from that of regular employees. Nevertheless, a relatively high number of Japanese people seem to accept the current situation. Surveys of views in regard to gender roles show Japan to be a largely conservative society with many women agreeing to an arrangement where men concentrate on their work and women on taking care of the household (Table 5.3).

However, diary entries have shown that non-regular employment is no longer limited to married women, students, and older semi-retired workers. There are several developments that increasingly challenge the prevailing understanding of non-regular employment

Table 5.3 Priorities of men and women in regard to work and family/ household (in %)

	Total	Men	Women	Young men	Young women
Men should prioritize work and women should prioritize family	44.0	46.6	41.6	36.9	38.0
Men should prioritize work and women should work and do household chores	20.3	15.5	24.6	12.1	19.2
Men and women should work and do household chores	18.1	18.3	17.8	24.8	24.0
Men should work and do household chores and women should prioritize family	7.0	8.0	6.1	11.7	9.2
Men and women should prioritize family	3.0	3.7	2.4	6.5	5.2
Men and women should prioritize work	3.7	3.4	4.1	3.7	3.3

Note: Answer to question: What lifestyle do you want to have?

Source: JILPT 2005a.

in Japan. The first is work for dispatch agencies. Data from the Ministry of Health, Labor and Welfare show a significant increase in the number of people sent by dispatch agencies, increasing from 395,000 people in 1999 to 1.52 million in 2006. This figure is calculated based on all employees having worked full-time, but in fact is spread over 3.2 million people that are continuously employed or registered with temporary dispatch agencies (MHLW 2007). The second development that goes hand in hand with the increase in dispatch workers is the increasing number of employees working for on-site subcontractors, often in the factories of major Japanese corporations. Chapter 2 has described this situation in some detail already and it was estimated that approximately 1 million manufacturing workers are employed like this. Finally, the third and most publicized development is an increase in so-called *freeter* – young, mostly single people who work in any of the above categories of non-regular employment.

Looking at motives, behaviors and characteristics of dispatch workers, Japan's largest temporary staffing company, Tempstaff, categorized its employees, and findings show that differences exist largely in accordance with age.

- 20 to 25 years old: reluctant to sign permanent contract with a company, wish to get some real world experience before committing to career, wish to test job market
- 25–40 years old: wish to change career track after a term of regular employment, unwilling to work for a company as a permanent staff member, looking for opportunities to use newly acquired skills
- 40 years +: work as temp staff as result of a restructured workplace, wish to use previously acquired skills in a new environment, wish for mid-career change, return to job market after having children (Tempstaff 2005).

The above categorization largely summarizes the motives provided earlier by diary writers. In its careful wording, the company acknowledges that some older people had to take up dispatch work, but it does not make the same acknowledgement for younger workers. Yet, another survey shows that 30% of female workers and about 15% of male workers took up employment with a temporary staffing agency because they could not find other employment (Chart 5.1).

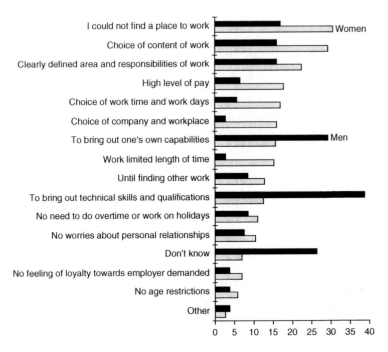

Chart 5.1 Reasons why people took up dispatch work (in %, up to three answers per employee)

Note: Survey conducted January 2001, 10,000 questionnaires, response rate 20.3%, for this question n = 879.

Source: Based on MHLW 2001.

Chart 5.1 also shows differences between men and women, with men mainly engaging in dispatch work to use their own capabilities and skills. Indeed, temporary staffing agencies employ people under two kinds of work arrangements. Most people are merely registered with the staffing company and only receive an employment contract when they are dispatched to a client. These are usually women and they are often used for relatively unqualified administrative and sales tasks. However, some employees are permanently employed with the staffing agency. These are usually male employees with professional skills, often in software development or information technology (Weathers 2001).

The term *freeter* overlaps with a number of other employment and social categories. *Freeter* can work as *arubaito,* part-timers or contract employees, for on-site subcontractors or dispatch companies. Considering the importance of the phenomenon it was probably necessary to introduce a new term, yet with terms like *arubaito* or part-timer already only vaguely defined, the introduction of the term *freeter* has further increased the opaqueness of Japanese labor markets.

In a White Paper on the National Lifestyle that considered the phenomenon, *freeter* were defined as people between 15 and 34 who, while not being married or studying, were working as part-timers or *arubaito* (inclusive of dispatch workers) or were unemployed, either having worked before or showing a willingness to work. Based on this definition, the *freeter* population stood at 4.17 people in 2001, an increase from about 1.82 million in 1990 (Naikakufu 2003). However, there is disagreement among the various institutions about the correct definition of *freeter*. The White Paper on the Labor Economy estimated the *freeter* population in 2003 at "only" 2.17 million. Here *freeter* were defined as all employees between 15 and 35 years of age (excluding married women) who worked under the status of *freeter* or part-timer, and all those who were not doing housework or were in school and seeking work under the status of part-timer or *freeter* (Kosugi 2004). Looking at the two definitions the real number of *freeter* is probably in between the two figures. The diary entries show that ultimately it is the perceptions of people themselves that matter, and as such, a person who is on a limited contract with a subcontractor or a person who is working full-time at a dispatch agency client might well be regarded as a *freeter*.

The Japanese Institute of Labor Policy and Training studied the issue of *freeter* intensively. Its researchers, especially Reiko Kosugi, grouped young people engaging in irregular employment into three categories according to their behavior and motives (JIL 2001).

- Moratorium-style: People who engage in contingent work until they find the right kind of work because they have not yet made up their mind about what they want to do, or want to have more freedom than regular employees. Members of this group are often school or university dropouts or young people who have failed entrance exams for the next level of education. Another type of person in this group is those who have quit working as regular employees after a short period of time due to problems in working conditions or human relationships at their workplaces. Due to their negative experiences they do not want to return immediately to regular employment.

• Forced-style: People who want to find work as regular employees but cannot find such employment and therefore have to engage in irregular work to support themselves. Also people who are waiting to take the next step in their education and have to support themselves or save for their education costs. Finally, those who are preoccupied with private problems, but still have to work.

• Pursuing-a-dream-style: People who engage in irregular work to finance the pursuit of their dreams, for example to become a rock musician by practicing with a band, or an actor by going to acting school. Others see their work as an apprenticeship or a way to eventually becoming freelancers, for example by assisting craftsmen, artists or designers.

Categorizing *freeter* into the three styles, JILPT found that 46.9% fell into the moratorium-style group and 39.4% fell into the involuntary group. Accordingly, the third group, which comes closest to the initially popular romanticized perception of the *freeter* – people working as non-regular employees to gain the time and resources to pursue their dreams – only accounted for 13.7% (JIL 2001). JILPT's results were largely confirmed in a survey by Recruit Works Institute (Chart 5.2). The study showed the main reasons for people becoming *freeter* were flexibility in terms of working hours, the possibility of engaging in pursuits outside work, the unwillingness to dedicate to a company, and finally indecisiveness concerning future work. Results also showed some significant differences between men and women, with some men trying to establish themselves as independent professionals.

Different skill levels have already been mentioned as an explanation for income discrepancies. Indeed, in its survey on working persons in 2004, Works Institute found significant differences in computer literacy between *freeter* and regular employees with 46% of male *freeter*, 49% of female *freeter* and 60% of female part-timers

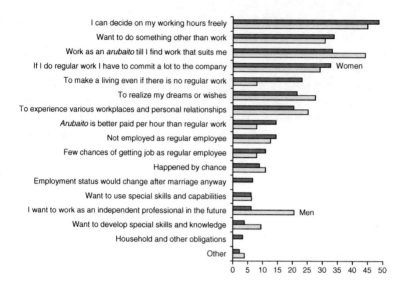

Chart 5.2   Reasons for people in the *freeter* group to take up work as *arubaito* (multiple answers in %)

Note: January and February 2000, people who worked in the category of *arubaito* aged up to 30 years old, except students and housewives, inclusive of dispatch and contract employees, n=308, men = 121, women = 187.

Source: adapted and translated from: *Arubaito no shūrō nado ni kan suru chōsa – furiitaa no ishiki-hatarikata no jittai ni tsuite* [Survey concerning the work and other issues of *arubaito* – about the attitudes and the work situation of *freeter*], 2000, p. 7. Recruit CO., LTD – Works Institute. http://www.works-i.com

admitting to the fact that they could not use a computer at all (regular employees 26%) (Kurosawa 2004). This ran counter to one of the popular images and perceptions of *freeter*, namely that many *freeter* were people who were very comfortable with technological developments and therefore could use such skills to make a living.

5.3   Living with anxieties

The previous section focused on motivations and pressures causing people to take up non-regular work, but diary writers have at the same time already addressed some of the anxieties that come with not being employed long-term. In the following, these anxieties will be taken up in more detail.

> *11 June 2004 – Today's work was the same as usual at the television assembly plant. But it was not the same in pre-testing; I was rotated to the assembly line. I have only worked on the line once before, more than half a year ago. Work on the line does not deliver much satisfaction so I was tense from the beginning. [Six days later she continues:] 17 June 2004: Because the dispatch work is on contract it is only limited and the income is unstable. On Tuesday and Friday I got work, today and tomorrow there is no work. But it helps in terms of spiritual and bodily strength.*[91]

The above author describes her work for a subcontractor in a television plant and is only hired on a daily basis. Another writer working in a white-collar administrative position voices similar sentiments and also shows that despite the earlier comments of some diary writers about the independence of dispatch work, some dispatch workers are not in control of their work content after all.

> *14 March 2003 – At the moment it is work that I am most dissatisfied with. I am a dispatch worker who nervously lives with monthly fluctuations in salary. I am working as a dispatch worker for a certain company. My work is largely administrative work ... Sometimes I am working 5 times a month, sometimes 12 times. The days are also irregular, work comes in suddenly ... But now I have been sent to branch Z, where no one wants to work. The boss of that branch is the worst. We are regularly requested to do work outside our normal work. Of course, this is the work of the people normally working in the Z branch. Tasks like shopping, cleaning, running errands, delivering and various others.*[92]

The next writer is afraid about the consequences of having fallen ill.

> *2 November 2004 – Caught a cold ... I have not been to work for two days in a row because I wasn't feeling well. Being a contract worker, this is a situation where one worries about what will happen? I am treading on thin ice. What fate faces a guy who has problems with attendance? Dismissal. One could say that since I am not feeling well, I cannot help it ... But it seems that a professional should go to work even when he is*

on his knees. ...In the future I will never rest, and I must try as much as possible to work like a pro. One can call this self-management, but how can one manage when one catches a cold or becomes ill?[93]

Another worker expresses his worries about the long-term consequences of working for a sub-contractor in manufacturing.

2 July 2004 – Worries concerning the future casting a shadow. Following up on yesterday's entry; around lunchtime, I went over to the factory to take a look at the workplace. In terms of the environment, the air-conditioning is effective and the work is not that difficult. (Getting the parts of the right kind and number as specified on the order slip and dropping them onto the conveyor belt)... While the work and the treatment were fine, various points weighed on my mind. There is no bonus (because it is work as a contract employee), and from now on there will not be the safety I had when I worked as a regular employee... With the number of contract employees and dispatch employees currently increasing, unfortunately regular employee positions seem to be reserved for managerial workers. But being a contract employee or a dispatch employee, for 10, for 20 years, will I always have work...? Can I do things like borrow money and build a house? Worries about the future cast a shadow.[94]

The excerpt below summarizes many of the anxieties that come with engaging in irregular work. While earlier diary writers have described not having to develop any attachment and commitment to their workplace as an advantage of dispatch work, the blog writer still faces the dilemma that after having worked at her company for some time, she has become attached to her workplace and does not want to leave.

31 July 2003 – On being a dispatch worker...: I arrived at the company and opened my mail and there was an appointment for a meeting with the most important person in the team in which I am currently working. I have not talked to him before. What are we going to talk about? I remembered!!! I'm only a dispatch worker. When I think about it, it is time for my contract renewal. Wah...is this finally the end of the contract?? ...Sure enough, it was very painful. The meeting was called because they only want to have two dispatch workers instead of the current four. My contract will be extended for another month. It seems that this is what everyone was told.

Advantages of dispatch work: If one dislikes it, one can quit easily. The responsibility is not as heavy as that of a regular employee. It is possible to detach oneself.

Disadvantages: It's frightening that one doesn't know when the contract will end. One is treated with disrespect. No bonus.

When one has found a place one likes, it is hard to be a dispatch worker. Even if one wants to stay, because of circumstances one often cannot do so. I like my present company. I want to stay but it seems difficult ... I must think of the future. It is very difficult to find work as a regular employee at my age. It's not as if there is much that I can do. It's scary.[95]

Finally, there is a statement by a self-declared high-tech *freeter* who, because of his qualifications, does not seem to share the anxieties of many of his fellow co-workers in irregular employment positions.

2 January 2004 – High-tech "freeter": Actually, while still on the current job, I am already thinking of working elsewhere and I am looking for work. As for the current job, if I produce results, afterwards things will be fine and there will not be much need for me to come any longer. It will be sufficient for one person just to come in on the weekends. Foolish? You may think so, but I have developed into a person who really produces proper results. But when the results materialize, the work comes to an end ... In April and May I intend to pick a place with good conditions. As a high-tech "freeter" I am not concerned about lifetime employment.[96]

The excerpts have shown the complexities involved when discussing people's motivations for engaging in non-regular work, and have contrasted them with the anxieties people face after taking up this sort of employment. Obviously people engage in non-regular employment for various reasons. Some do so because they cannot find other work; others because they find that this type of work corresponds to other obligations or allows them to pursue other interests. Yet others see non-regular work as a chance to experience different kinds of work and to eventually find a workplace that suits them. Finally, there are people who see non-regular work as an alternative to regular work, citing the restrictions and conditions that come with being a regular worker, such as having to work as a generalist with no say in regard to work content. Some people also do not want to become part of the tight networks of human relationships that exist in Japanese corporations.

In terms of anxieties of people working as non-regular employees the comments of blog authors probably do not need further substantiation. Being treated differently in terms of pay, bonuses and workplace security must clearly lead to corresponding anxieties. Nevertheless, people have also been surveyed in terms of the anxieties of non-regular employment (Chart 5.3). Not surprisingly people in regular employment were the most satisfied with their job security; though considering the high importance usually attributed to lifetime employment in Japanese corporations one would expect an even higher level of satisfaction here. Dispatch workers were the least satisfied, followed by the group of part-timers working long hours and then those working shorter hours.

The fact that part-timers who work short hours were relatively satisfied with their job security can be attributed to two points. First,

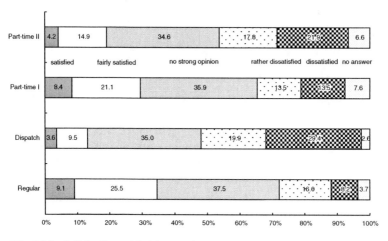

Chart 5.3 Satisfaction with job security
Note: part-time I = working short hours, part-time II = others.
Source: JILPT 2004b: 341.

such part-timers usually perform relatively simple, low paid jobs, often in service industries or retailing. Since these sectors have a constant demand for people, part-time employees do not have to worry too much about finding a new job if they lose their current one. Secondly, the nature of their jobs and their low pay does not make them prone to restructuring or reorganization. Indeed, statistics show that many part-timers have been with one company for a long time, with contracts being renewed so regularly that even judicial courts have supported part-timers who have claimed that their contracts should be regarded as quasi-permanent.

Recruit Works Institute further surveyed *freeter* working in the employment category of *arubaito* about the advantages and disadvantages of their type of employment (Chart 5.4). Again respondents

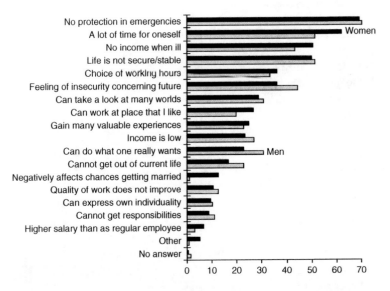

Chart 5.4 Merits and demerits of *arubaito* work as seen by *freeter* (multiple answers in %)

Note: January and February 2000, people who work in the category of *arubaito* aged up to 30 years old, except students and housewives, including dispatch and contract employees, n=308, men = 121, women = 187.

Source: Adapted and translated from: *Arubaito no shūrō nado ni kan suru chōsa – furiitaa no ishiki-hatarikata no jittai ni tsuite* [Survey concerning the work and other issues of *arubaito* – about the attitudes and the work situation of *freeter*], 2000, p. 38. Recruit CO., LTD – Works Institute. http://www.works-i.com

pointed to advantages of their work such as the freedom in terms of time and work content and the possibility of gaining experience in a variety of occupations. At the same time though, answers revealed major worries concerning the security of workplaces and especially protection in emergency situations such as prolonged illness and the inability to work. Differences between men and women were of lower importance here, but some men said that working as a *freeter* might harm their prospects of getting married. Interestingly, women did not have such worries at all, pointing to the still very strong difference in expectations based on gender in Japan.

Earlier, it was outlined that the situation in terms of contingent work in Japan was sometimes explained by differences in employees' priorities as well as qualifications. Surveys have indeed shown that such differences exist, yet also that this is not the case for everyone. Thus Osawa (2001: 196) argued as follows in response to an argument by Aoki:

> *Full-time part-timers who work as long hours as regular employees, stay with the company for just as many years as regulars, yet are paid much lower wages and hence pay the costs of growth? Real part-timers who work shorter hours than regular workers, but whose energy results in a bigger contribution to the firm's activities? Such people simply do not exist in the Aoki model. The model is an imaginary world, far removed from reality.*

Heidi Gottfried (2002: 247–248) in a reply to articles by Satō, Osawa and Weathers (all 2001) argues that the different views on the underlying causes of non-regular employment and differences in treatment actually do not contradict each other but just focus on different aspects of the same problem:

> *Clearly one must understand that workers exercise personal choice (supply side considerations), and that these choices occur within the context of corporate actions (demand-side considerations). What this research indicates is that corporate choices are not only driven by market forces; state policies create arenas for employment practices. Likewise, individual decisions may not be as optional as presumed.*

Consequently Gottfried expresses some weariness with the ongoing debate concerning the motivations of non-regular employees and differences in their treatment, and instead outlines questions that she regards as being of higher importance (2002: 248):

> *What are the implications of increasing individualization of employment relationships and diversification of employment contracts? Will shifting employment statuses lead to permanent disadvantages and greater inequalities? How will tenuous job attachments without formal membership of an organization affect identities? How will discontinuities and shifting career paths affect the meaning of work in young people's lives? What effect will non-standard employment relationships have on social security systems and the distribution of risks?*

Strongly supporting Gottfried's assessment that to understand the situation of non-regularly employed workers in Japan one must look beyond motives and remuneration, the next chapter considers the actual situation of non-regular employees in their workplaces.

6
Working as a
Non-Regular Employee

*6 July 2004 – Today was the last day of three consecutive full
nights of arubaito. I worked for a contractor of a certain large
home electronics manufacturer, on the production line in the factory ... While doing so there were things that caught my eye. First:
The image one has of the production and assembly of hand phones
is of a large machine that assembles the items making "bing and
bang" noises. But, what I actually saw came as a surprise!! It
really is production by hand. While we were doing it, since it is
line production, I did not see the final product, but only respect-
fully put five parts together. Second: In terms of being a freeter it
was a big, unpleasant surprise. For me, who has a dream, it is
different, but having to do work like this just to survive, I glumly
thought that this must be hard. ... Third: Among the people working in the factory, about 10% of the arubaito caught my interest.
They have an important role in supervision. Those freeter work all
day long (under the arubaito dispatch system), and drive production by forming teams and instructing new people. ... What to call
this? For this factory eventually the picture emerged, that "assembly line production is impossible without freeter." Well, without
dispatch arubaito they would be able to do something (it was like
that in the past after all), but now the production method described
above has become the basis for companies' profits ... So, weren't
freeter portrayed on television as bad?*[97]

Companies are increasingly relying on non-regular employees in their
operations, and as the above blog entry outlines, are even assigning

some of them leadership roles. Thus, when discussing non-regular work it is necessary to take a closer look at the actual work situation of non-regular employees. With non-regular employment becoming a long-term situation for many employees, it is also important to ask whether it can still become a starting point for building a career. This chapter takes up these two issues and then goes on to discuss the situation of Japan's growing non-regular workforce within over-all changes in labor markets in Japan and other countries.

6.1   Conflicting motivations and expectations

29 October 2003 – Over New Year none of the part-timers will be around, so we have to use regular employees, freeter and arubaito. So I have to train them from now on. It seems as if my days will continue to be busy, but since there are many female employees to be trained this is fine and they are also close to my age. Saying so, the proportion of female employees is very high in this workplace. One of the three regular employees is a woman, then there are more than 10 part-timers and arubaito, but only one of them is male. I don't have an interest in housewives, so I won't talk about the part-timers, but there are many young girls among the arubaito, so it is quite enjoyable. There are also students from girls' schools and women's universities ... But, while one thinks of it as being enjoyable, one also needs to think about the other side; if one is disliked by the women's camp, it gets tough. Really, there are part-timers who just spread rumors each time they open their mouth. I have written about it before. There was a kid who joined the company with me who was badmouthed by the part-timers, lost his spirit and had to quit.[98]

The above diary entry introduces the social aspects of Japanese workplaces. The writer above is a young manager in a retail store, where the majority of people under his supervision are contingent employees, most of them middle-aged female part-timers. With many regular employees of retail companies spending the first years of their career in actual store management, the young male worker in his first year is not the only employee reporting in his diary about difficulties he faces by suddenly having to supervise a group of part-timers. In the next diary entry, written on the same day, the same writer outlines the work situation in his store further. As pointed out, due to family obligations female part-timers are normally not available during holidays, vacation periods and early and late hours of business. He therefore welcomes the increasing availability of *freeter* since not only are they cheap but they have no family obligations and are thus deployable in the same or even in a more flexible manner than regular employees.

> *29 October 2003 – Not that I look down on freeter, but among "freeter" there are all sorts. I want to employ good freeter from now on, but it happens that the impression given during the interview may be different from the actual impression when working. Of course, it is up to me in the position of supervisor to make use of them.*
>
> *By the way, in my company, the ranking goes like this: Regular employees> freeter> Part-timer> arubaito. Compared to part-timers, freeter have less of a sense of life, so though they may be oblivious to the value of competition, they are less restricted in terms of working hours and can thereby be used as quasi-[regular] employees.*
>
> *The work content is also on a par with that of regular employees, and so are days off at 8 to 9 days per month. I think they are the true part-timers. Even so, their hourly pay is lower than that of us regular employees, really not much of a difference when compared with that of arubaito. Perhaps, this is unprofitable part-time work. But for people who enjoy retailing it must be enjoyable.[99]*

The impression that dispatch and contract employees are becoming more and more important is reinforced by the next diary writer.

> *11 June 2003 – It's tough to remember my new work. Today is my third day of training. I'm what they call a "factory lady" (already past the age of being a lady though). I've been working as a dispatch worker for a year but now I'm doing machine operator work alongside the regular employees...In September, another line will be fully operational. When that happens, it is expected that the regular employees will become fully occupied, so we dispatch workers will be marked out to help. Eh. But to make the dispatch workers do the same work as the regular workers, better say to entrust it to them, this means that they have confidence in us, doesn't it? Thinking of this, I feel the energy welling up to work tomorrow.[100]*

While the above diary writer feels motivated by the fact that she was entrusted with the same tasks as regular employees, the writer of the next blog excerpt wonders why he had to work more than regular employees and what the logic and economic rationality behind this arrangement was.

> *6 January 2001 – Today's diary: Recently I have been busy at work ... Well, it cannot be helped because it has become important to prepare all sorts of documents to submit to each city, town and village, to calculate salaries and to administer the merger. I leave the company after 10 pm ... You might say "isn't that still early?" but everyone around me has already left by then, including my boss of course. Well, I am a dispatch worker after all, but ... When they make me work overtime, this simply becomes a loss for the company, but ... Why do I have to work more than the regular employees? ... Not only that, important work.*[101]

Finally a dispatch employee finds herself with the responsibility to train other employees upon leaving her current assignment, a process that frequently takes place in companies that employ a large number of dispatch workers.

> *3 February 2004 – I was going to finish work here soon, but due to company circumstances I will be extended to March and I am angry. Talking about this reminds me that there were also many problems when I quit the company where I was a regular employee ... (faraway look) ... I was to leave at the end of March, but because the new employee had not finished training I had to continue part-time in April (anger). Before leaving, you get twice as busy as usual (tired). After I quit as a regular employee, I have been at about four companies as a dispatch worker. No matter how often this happens to me, each time it is tiring to resign. Without doubt, it is very tiring to teach people.*[102]

That dispatch workers and other non-regularly employed workers do not just perform simple tasks gives employees some leverage over their employers.

> *7 March 2003 – Just when things had calmed down, in the afternoon a manager of the dispatch agency came round to take a look at how things were. What he said was that the company wants us to stay for another*

month. A girl who had joined at the same time as me seems, however, to have broken away and refused. She did not see much merit in staying, with hourly wages being low and the need to cover one's own commuting costs. For the same reason, I will avoid answering and will try to negotiate an increase in the hourly wage. When, from April onwards, totally new people have to come in for only one month, productivity will surely worsen and so a situation will occur where they will want me to stay, since I am a bit more experienced. Speaking of the cards the dispatch company is holding, they also have to be concerned about the future relationship with the client company.[103]

It was shown earlier that some employees took up non-regular employment expecting that employers would demand less from them than from regular employees. In reality this does not always seem to be the case.

28 July 2004 – But, suddenly it seems that there will be a study session about ISO at 5 pm for 30 minutes. Now look, normally isn't it just the regular employees that take part in such things. Why do contract employees have to be included in everything here? Also, the habit of talking for a long time; one wants to shout angrily "let's all go to sleep." If they say that it will last 30 minutes, it will last one hour. There is no pay for the 30 minutes. I don't feel like doing free overtime for such a company.[104]

The following blog writer similarly complained about having to be in the workplace outside working hours. Being paid by the hour she did not accept extra demands by the company.

14 April 2003 – Each day, five minutes before we begin work there is a morning assembly. There is no pay for this. Another woman has said: "Isn't it true that in every company one has to come early to do things like cleaning up and watering the flowers? We do not have to do such things here, so we have the 5-minute morning assembly." Of course, I am happy to participate in the morning assembly 5 minutes before work. But, the problem is, there is no pay for this. And, we only work for 3 to 4 hours as part-timers every day. There are no longer life-long employees like during the age of Hara Setsuko [Actress famous in the 1940s and 1950s].[105]

A writer working in a call center gives an account of his reaction when asked by his supervisor to work overtime on short notice.

> *12 January 2004 – Isn't that stupid? In my workplace, 99% are agency workers. Only the head of the center is a regular employee. I had just thought "now let's go home," when he said "The number of calls has increased, you cannot go home." But, didn't I finish my working hours? And, isn't it true that there is no payment for overtime?*
>
> *I: "Excuse me I have things to do" I said as I got up to leave.*
>
> *Supervisor: "All are staying back. You want to be the only one to leave?"*
>
> *I: "Yes, my working hours are up and even if I do overtime there is no overtime payment."*
>
> *Supervisor: "This cannot be."*
>
> *I: "Why not? In a workplace where there are no regular employees, no bonuses, no increase in hourly pay, and no overtime pay you cannot expect personal sacrifice."*
>
> *Supervisor: "... You can leave," (with an extremely furious look).*
>
> *I: "Good bye, see you tomorrow" (with smile).*
>
> *So, have I said something wrong?*[106]

The writer of the following diary entry describes his workplace favorably overall. However, he complains about the lack of a bonus and concludes that thus there is no reason for him to stay long-term at the company.

> *4 September 2002 – The work environment: Because it is work in a clean room, it is probably not polluted at all. The air-conditioning is also perfect, a good environment I think. The work is the best of the work I have done so far. When I think about the balance of my hourly pay and the difficulty of work, it looks like the best cost-performance so far. Although it is factory work, it is close to deskwork ... I am not a regular employee, but work contract on dispatch, meaning I am employed through a worker rental agency. Therefore, the income depends on the contract company. That is roughly 7,000 to 8,500 yen per day, with*

overtime paid separately. So far so good, but because there is no bonus ((((;°Д°)))♭ wobbling and shivering, there is no merit in working here for a long time.[107]

Finally, a contract employee provides his views on a company that largely uses non-regular employees and he sees this fact as being, to a large degree, responsible for the poor state it is in.

> *6 February 2004 – What is "normal?" I think that the company I am currently contracted to is the weirdest workplace so far compared to the previous ones. There are only a small number of employees and most of them are dispatch or contract staff. Of course, the superiors are also like this and so the place has sunk into a state of slackness. Twenty people joined at the same time as me, but one resigned immediately and this month two more have resigned. Every month someone leaves. It feels as if the remaining staff falls into just two groups. Either people who welcome slackness, or the others, those who have changed workplaces too often.*[108]

The perception that non-regular employees have a different sense of loyalty was also expressed by some of their co-workers and supervisors.

> *5 November 2003 – In spite of this calm season, work has been increasing with a vengeance. In the end, an older male dispatch worker said that the work was tough and he abandoned his badly designed piece and quit. As the dispatch workers' regional manager, I cannot help but feel that the dispatch company has been amiss in its education. It may be unfair to those dispatch workers who work hard but I thought "After all, dispatch workers don't feel that it is their company, so they have a weak sense of responsibility." Life is not so easy that one can just run away if one fails.*

> *What to complain about: speaking about the assignment of work and duties by the company, it is problematic that work entrusted was not matched to the worker's abilities. This is dangerous, so I kept asking for experienced personnel to be sent quickly, increasing the number of personnel and changing workers, but I was told "Please let them try hard and wait a bit longer." Such irresponsible thinking ended up causing trouble even for the customers.*[109]

While the diary writer above also considers the dispatch company at fault by not taking enough care in selecting workers, the diary writer below simply attributes what he perceives as a poor work attitude to the young age of the employees dispatched to his company.

> *12 November 2003 – Hah, dispatch ... Dispatch workers can't be used. Well, they are young, so they should enjoy themselves (bitter laugh). Already, everyone judges them negatively. As for me, today I ended up doing overtime to clear up work that two dispatch workers (18 or 19-year-old modern young ladies) have left behind (bitter laugh). Aah, I didn't want to sound like this. Those girls surely are not aware that they are receiving money for doing work.*[110]

However, another writer contradicts this statement by describing her work experience with dispatch workers as enjoyable, especially lauding their professional attitude.

> *25 February 2002 – Until now, I have not worked with dispatch workers, but it is enjoyable. This is because, compared to normal employees, these are people with a professional attitude.*[111]

The blog entry below is by a supervisor who tried to treat dispatch workers the same way as normal employees, recognizing that they also needed to be trained and motivated, although he was not sure how to do so.

> *26 November 2003 – Can I also manage dispatch workers like this? Mr. O's method is to let dispatch workers finish work step by step according to their training schedule. By the way, colleagues other than Mr. O. direct everything themselves and just assign simple tasks to dispatch workers. In other words, training of dispatch workers (developing them) is not really carried out. Of course, one can feel a certain sense of accomplishment, but ... I am thinking of developing the abilities and experience of the dispatch workers working under me and giving them work in a way that gives them a sense of meaning. But this is very difficult.*[112]

Having to deal with a larger number of non-regular employees is clearly a challenge to supervisors. In the following diary entry the author expresses the need to come up with ways to maintain quality and reliability while at the same time managing a diverse workforce.

> *3 July 2003 – From now on I have to prepare materials for "kaizen" [continuous improvement] activities. With people from various levels around, like dispatch workers, contract workers and subcontractors, we need to establish a system that produces products without confusion and mistakes. At the same time, by using whatever technical skills we have, we must create products that other competitors cannot copy. For companies like ours, which are not so big, achieving these two feats is necessary if we want to continue to exist and have our manufacturing base in Japan.*[113]

In the following entry an employee describes her position in a multi-level system of employment and supervision. Her work contract is with a dispatch company that hired her out to an Internet provider. The Internet service provider then sent her to retail stores to promote its services, where, since customers were not aware of this situation, she also had to engage in advising customers about other products.

> *20 September 2003 – Here comes discontent! I have become a dispatch worker for a certain human resources dispatch company, and so I have been dispatched to work as a salesperson for a certain ADSL provider. On top of that, sales for the ADSL provider are conducted at a certain large electric appliances store. As a result, my actual workplace is at this large electric appliances store, and while my main duty is to work at the application counter for ADSL, it is also common that I have to serve customers in the store if they want something else…Considering how it has come to this situation, the business partner of the dispatch company is the ADSL provider, and then again the ADSL provider is the business partner of the electric appliances store.*[114]

The status of dispatch workers in corporations thus is often not entirely clear, as the following entry by a writer shows. She expresses her empathy with a dispatch worker who is suddenly being discriminated against.

> *22 June 2003 – We had our company excursion on Saturday. [The day before] just when I wanted to say "Let's enjoy ourselves" an incident occurred. Upon leaving the company on Friday our president said to*

Ms. N, a dispatch worker. "Since you are a dispatch worker, you will have to pay half the fee for this company excursion, so please pay when we have returned from our trip." Of course this will be about 10,000 yen. Wait a moment. So far, dispatch workers have participated at the expense of the company. This cannot happen on such short notice. Shouldn't one say something like this earlier?[115]

Finally, we see dispatch workers becoming part of the informal organization of a company, with regular employees developing an attachment to them that goes beyond the work relationship. The excerpt below again demonstrates the complexity of personnel movements taking place in Japanese corporations, with one group of dispatch employees being exchanged for another.

27 December 2003 – Goodbye. The dispatch workers who have worked for one year at my workplace have this time been made to leave. Absurdly, the reason was the intervention of the dispatch company that belongs to our own company group. It wanted work for its own dispatch workers, and so our own employment plan has become obsolete... We have been to Disneyland together, have exchanged views at presentations, and have become quite close. In a word: this puts the finishing touch to boredom.[116]

The above blog entries introduced the various issues that arise when working as a non-regular employee or when working with or even managing non-regular employees. Obviously, non-regular employees have assumed an important role within many Japanese corporations. Companies have become dependent on them and it is thus impossible to still regard them merely as fringe or contingent employees. Conflict seems to occur, however, when employers demand that dispatch employees show engagement that goes beyond the level that they are prepared to give.

Companies have shown awareness about the fact that the increase in non-regular employees poses challenges for their current management methods. In a survey by Works Institute (2004a) companies recognized a number of factors, among them the need to explain changes to stakeholders such as existing employees, unions and customers, problems with the motivation of existing employees, the need to reassign tasks to employees whose tasks were taken up by non-regular employees, and finally the training of non-regular employees as well as their supervisors (Table 6.1).

Table 6.1 Problems with the employment of non-regular employees by type of non-regular employment (in %)

	Contract	Part-timer/ arubaito	Dispatch	Individual subcontract	Subcontract/ outsourcing
Number of companies answering	676	646	606	168	205
Problems in %					
Need to explain to employees	18.0	18.7	18.8	20.2	24.9
Need to explain to customers	4.0	4.2	3.6	6.5	5.4
Consulting with unions	4.7	4.0	5.4	6.0	8.8
Reassigning employees	11.8	11.0	11.6	13.7	14.6
Effects on existing employees' motivation	11.2	11.5	11.1	13.7	13.2
Finding non-regular employees	13.2	13.3	14.4	18.5	18.5
Training non-regular employees	16.4	16.7	17.0	16.7	22.9
Training supervisors	11.4	12.5	11.2	11.9	14.6
No answer	48.7	47.5	47.5	37.5	37.6

Note: Survey of 20,000 companies, response 1,168 companies, July and August 2003.

Source: Adapted and translated from: *Posuto seika shūgi jidai no jinzai manejimento o kangaeru – Works jinzai manejimento chōsa 2003* [Thinking about the personnel management of the post-merit principle era – Works Personnel Management Survey 2003], 2004. Recruit CO., LTD – Works Institute. http://www.works-i.com

The survey also went one step further and asked for information on more concrete problems. Here a relatively high number of companies responded that management had become more complex (16.3%), while a smaller number of companies reported other problems such as dissatisfaction of existing employees (6.5%); a decline in the quality of products or services (6.5%); problems motivating external personnel (5.0%); cases where customers had voiced their discontent (3.3%); a drop in productivity (2.8%); or a worsening in the workplace atmosphere (1.9%) (Works Institute 2004a).

Thus, most of the problems mentioned in the above blog excerpts also appear in empirical surveys. Yet, it is difficult to judge their relevance. Is the occurrence of a decline in the quality of products and services as stated by 6.5% of companies significant or not? In addition, the figures are based on the perceptions of those in charge of personnel departments, with little involvement in the actual workplaces.

Surveys of people closer to the actual workplace showed results of higher significance. The Whitepaper of Manufacturing for the year 2004 included a survey of 413 respondents from the manufacturing industries. The survey results first stressed some success in the introduction of more non-regular employees. A total of 55.2% of companies responded that through the use of subcontractors and other forms of non-regular work in their factories they had indeed increased their competitiveness by realizing lower costs and greater flexibility. However, 52.8% of survey participants also voiced fears that the shift towards a higher share of non-regular employees would hurt them in the long run in terms of developing technically skilled personnel. Also, 39% voiced apprehension concerning the control of production processes and quality control of products since it was no longer regular employees who were performing such tasks. However, 15.7% of respondents also cited positive experiences in terms of maintaining quality levels. They argued that they were now able to procure the right personnel in a timely manner without having to overstretch their existing workforces in times of high demand, this having been the cause of drops in quality in the past (KSS/KRS/MKS, 2004).

A detailed survey of factory managers of companies listed on the first section of the Tokyo Stock Exchange (response by 227 companies) was carried out by Nikkei Business in August 2004. Here 54.2% of respondents said they felt that strength in production on the shop floor had decreased, while 40.1% answered that this was not the case. Those that reported a decrease in strength pointed to symptoms such as the occurrence of production mismatches (42.3%); the occurrence of problems in safety management through improper designation of functions or untidy workplaces (26.8%); an increase in the rate of product defects (26.0%); recent occurrences of accidents or cases of confusion in the production process (26.0%); and finally fears about the sinking morale of employees and problems with punctuality and absenteeism (6.5%).

Factory managers related this development to a number of underlying factors such as workers lacking knowledge and experience due to insufficiencies in training systems and the diffusion of technical skills (71.5%); supervisors in charge of the actual production process being overloaded due to the reorganization of production systems and a decrease in personnel due to restructuring (39.8%); an increase in the number of workers lacking the right professional attitude or spirit (37.4%); an increased dependence on collaborating companies and external providers, resulting in a decrease in actual skills on the shop floor (33.3%); the ageing of production equipment, with machines requiring more maintenance and care and increasing the chances of accidents (17.9%); manuals detailing production processes and safety procedures becoming outdated (13.8%); and finally a lack of capacity and personnel while production output was increased (12.2%) (Hanami and Saito 2004).

Finally, dispatch work was taken up in a comprehensive company survey by the Ministry of Health, Labor and Welfare. The wish list of receiving companies towards dispatch workers, dispatch agencies and governmental regulators shows some interesting contradictions when compared to the motivations of dispatch workers (Table 6.2). While many people chose dispatch work because they wanted to work in their narrow area of specialization and/or did not want to get too involved with workplace matters, employers asked dispatch workers for greater adaptability towards the workplace or to broaden and deepen their skills. Dispatch agencies were asked to match workplaces and skills better and also to train their employees, while the government was asked to extend the maximum length that dispatch employees could work for one company.

Table 6.2   Wishes of receiving companies concerning dispatch work

Towards dispatch workers	%
Increase skills	58.6
More adaptability towards workplace	41.5
Widen scope of work	22.7
Keep to regulations in regard to working hours and other regulations	19.1
Work outside working hours and on vacation days	6.2
Towards dispatch agencies	
Raise level of knowledge and skills of employees	49.7
Properly match knowledge of employees and demands	43.7
Strengthen contact with workplaces	19.8
Comply with dispatch contract	18.2
Explain working conditions to employee as outlined by receiving side	12.6
Have grievance counseling	10.1
Properly assign persons in charge of dispatch employees	10.0
Towards government regulators	
Review regulations on maximum length of deployment	49.6
Provide proper education and training	24.3
Ease inclusion of dispatch workers into social and labor insurance	22.2
Come up with a proper public system of recognized qualifications and skills	18.8
Reduce areas that are closed to dispatch companies	17.4
Educate public on dispatch system	16.5

Note: Survey of 10,000 companies with dispatch workers, response rate 12.2%, 1223 companies, January 2001.
Source: MHLW 2001.

Thus, what employers were really looking for, were regular employees but at lower cost and with fewer obligations on their side, and indeed, many non-regular employees felt that they were performing the same tasks as regular employees. In the Works survey on non-regular employment, 22.4% of non-regular workers answered that in their workplace they had regular employees who did the same job as them, and 37.4% answered that there were regular employees who did largely the same job. Only 16.4% answered that this was not the case at all, while 23.8% admitted that they did not really understand the situation. The feeling that regular employees and non-regular employees performed the same tasks was highest among contract employees, followed by *freeter* and dispatch workers (Works Institute 2001).

Works Institute also asked about specific functions performed by non-regular employees and found that a significant number of non-regular employees were actually performing some sort of leadership role with some non-regular employees even guiding regular employees (Table 6.3). Here *freeter* were the most involved.

The area where the use of non-regular employees was most advanced was the service sector, especially retail stores and restaurants. Here, so-called part-timers have become the largest group of employees, with companies not being able to run their operations any longer without them. Honda (2004) of the JILPT, who has studied personnel policies in the service sector intensively, argues that part-timers were initially used in this sector to counter the uneven demand situation. However, companies later increasingly raised the proportion of part-timers to save on costs. To do so, companies came up with organizational structures that allowed operations to run with minimal use of regular employees. Thus the systematic utilization

Table 6.3 Advanced tasks performed by non-regular employees (multiple answers in %)

	Married part-timer	*Freeter*	Other *arubaito/* part-timer	Dispatch	Contract
Guide and train new employees	18.9	33.2	20.4	20.0	27.8
Assign and instruct employees other than regular employees	9.5	21.7	10.7	11.9	20.5
Play leadership role by raising spirit etc.	8.5	15.0	11.3	8.0	15.9
Assign and instruct regular employees	4.9	11.3	4.6	9.5	13.2
Do not do any of the above	73.2	56.8	68.1	70.3	58.3

Sources: Adapted and translated from: *Hitenkei koyō rōdōsha chōsa 2001* [Survey of workers in regard to irregular employment], 2001, p. 66. Recruit CO., LTD – Works Institute. http://www.works-i.com

of different groups of people willing to work as non-regular employees became important. This policy was outlined by some of the blog writers, for example the writer who argued that it was most advantageous for organizations to employ *freeter*.

Honda (2004) thus argues that the process that saw part-timers becoming the main focus of employment policies developed in two dimensions. The quantitative dimension describes an increase in the proportion of non-regular employees compared to employees overall. The qualitative dimension describes non-regular employees taking over more and more sophisticated tasks that were previously performed by regular employees and even becoming active in small group activities to raise productivity.

Morishima and Shimanuki (2005) of Hitotsubashi University relate problems that temporary dispatch employees experienced in their workplaces to flaws in personnel management. They argue that a combination of several factors, such as being responsible to two employers, a mismatch of information between the dispatch agency and the client company, and finally the short-term perspective of many employees themselves, leads to a situation where employees are not properly trained, evaluated, or remunerated and not properly matched to their workplaces. This eventually leads to a decline in the willingness of dispatch workers to work and perform.

Similarly, Fujimoto and Kimura (2005) look at the situation in the on-site contract industry. Identifying various corporate business models, they find that companies shared one characteristic, a relatively low emphasis on the development of human resources. Workers were rotated regularly, but this was done to keep them employed and to meet demands of various clients, and not with the purpose of developing their skills further. Similarly, most companies did not raise salaries based on the performance of workers and would only do so if client companies agreed to an increase in fees. Fujimura and Kimura largely hold client companies responsible for this situation with clients usually looking only at costs and not at the quality of personnel offered by dispatch agencies or contractors or the human resource management policies that they employ.

Weathers (2001), in a qualitative study on the situation of temporary workers, paints a relatively dark picture of the industry, with workers having to accept a high level of discrimination in workplaces and differences in treatment, not only in terms of gender, but also due to their workplace status and age. He found a tendency among client companies to select dispatch employees by appearance and age. In terms of age of female employees he reports that clients set age restrictions, so that regularly employed women did not have to supervise and instruct older women. He also found that dispatch employees were sometimes excluded from the use of certain company facilities and that they regularly had to perform tasks that went beyond their original job scope. Blog entries have largely been in accord with his claims, but on the other hand have also shown how some people have adjusted to their workplaces, wanted to stay with their companies and have found acceptance by regularly employed co-workers.

Ishihara and Shinozaki (2005) look at the question of whether non-regular workers accepted lower wage levels than regular employees, and argue that perceptions change over the course of employment. They outline several situations in which this happens and their findings mirror what some blog writers have outlined.

- Non-regular employees initially perceive wages as appropriate when they compare their own situation in terms of working hours, work content and responsibilities, with the situation of regular employees. However, this perception changes when non-regular employees stay longer, take on more responsibilities, and the complexity of their work increases.
- Non-regular employees cannot assess responsibilities and work content before taking up employment and only find out about the real content once they begin their work.
- Employees are not aware of monetary rewards for non-regular and regular employees and only find out about disadvantages after they take on the actual job.

Ishihara and Shinozaki went on to investigate the dissatisfaction of non-regular employees in terms of wage levels and found that it was especially female married part-time workers that accepted the wage gap while workers in other groups showed higher levels of dissatisfaction. They found that the level of job responsibility and skills were a deciding factor. *"For both voluntary and involuntary part-time workers, less on the job responsibility results in acceptance and a high level of required skills tends toward rejection with statistic significance"* (Ishihara and Shinozaki 2005: 71).

This issue leads to the next big question in terms of non-regular employment in Japan. If employees become dissatisfied with their own situation, are they able to switch to other modes of employment or is there room for development within their current mode of employment?

6.2   Developing a career?

16 February 2003 – I want to work towards getting a promotion. One and a half years ago I resigned from work, became a freeter and began to look for work that I wanted to do. I made a big effort to try out different jobs. As a result, this is the work that I like most. This workplace, and also the people. Only when one is young, can one afford to spend one and a half years thinking, I want to do what I like. Having rested for too long it is time to get working, since it has become a problem that I am not earning enough. But I won't go back into manufacturing. I want to work for a promotion because I really like this work. I want to aim at becoming a manager. All along I had thought that this was impossible for me. Since all our managers have graduated from university and I am just a high-school graduate, and moreover a fallen high-school graduate, I thought that I could not do it. But ...,[117]

The writer of the first diary entry reports that she has succeeded in her search for a workplace that suits her interests. Having decided to continue to work in the restaurant industry she later reports that she has found some support from her current superior in developing a career, despite lacking the educational qualifications she initially deemed necessary.

The next diary entry describes another case where non-regular employment paved the way to regular employment, though not everything seems to be going smoothly.

20 November 2003 – A friend of mine has become a regular employee after having been introduced through a dispatch company. She then had to change department, and the content of her work also changed to something totally outside her field. I had thought that the merit of dispatch work was that one could choose one's type of work. And also

I thought that the merit of being introduced through a dispatch com-
pany is that one can find out whether the company atmosphere and
the type of work really suit you. But she thinks this has been proved to
be absurd and has repeatedly called me to say that she wants to quit.
Just being on dispatch is fine; she wishes to continue the work she has
done so far.[118]

Though regular employment did not provide the satisfaction the
diary writer's friend wanted, she would probably still be envied
by many other temporarily employed blog writers who for various
reasons describe it as very difficult to find employment as regular
employees. The first blog author, despite performing well in his
workplace, faces the rigidities of a company that does not hire people
mid-career out of principle.

29 June 2003 – My current work has no connection to building a career.
The company where I currently work does not engage in mid-career hir-
ing at all. Therefore if I want to work, I need to look for a position as a
regular employee. Stress is building up. I am doing the same work as a
regular employee, but there are clear differences in terms of salary and
there is also discrimination.[119]

Another diary author reports concerns in terms of age. While having
doubts about whether she is really suited to do so, she would like to
become a regular employee. However, although only 35 years old,
she feels that her time is running out.

14 December 2003 – More or less while looking for a new job for the
next year, I have come to think that it would be good to become a regu-
lar employee. In three months I will be 35 years old and it seems that
because of this the path towards becoming a regular employee has
become extremely narrow. However, it is unlikely that people like me,
who hate things like management and hate following people around,
can become a full-time employee (...blow myself up...). Yet since I
have bought a comprehensive life insurance policy I have to search for
work...Next I should do a job that improves my skills a bit more [120]

In searching for work as regular employees, people face much competition, and some of this competition comes from fresh graduates,

as the writer of the next excerpt points out.

> *26 November 2003 – On the way back I went to my old school. I went to a talk on finding work. This year again, it seems to be tough, a lot of fresh graduates all striving hard. Today I have been thinking that I have really been born into a bad era. Lately, I have grown sick of the occupation of freeter. Really, I must get a good proper job. I have no money.*[121]

This raises the question of how companies view experience accumulated in non-regular work. The next diary writer reports on the harsh reservations she encountered in a job interview for a position as a regular employee. The person who interviewed her questioned her sincerity and angered the writer by largely attributing her interest in the job to the better remuneration that comes with regular employment.

> *22 October 2001 – Today, I went for an interview. Unexpectedly it was an interview with the president. I was surprised. Among the questions, what really hurt was: "You have been a dispatch worker until now, so why have you suddenly made up your mind to become a regular employee? Well, regular employees get bonuses, don't they?" It's not that I particularly wanted to be a dispatch worker! I couldn't find an opening as a regular employee for some time so I just did it for the time being. And I was still dissatisfied with the welfare benefits…It seems that the notification will come in a week. I am thinking what to do.*[122]

The next writer describes his reluctance to give up looking for a regular job. He does not want to follow the advice of his parents to start his career in non-regular employment, since companies he has had interviews with did not show interest in the experience he has gained in the various part-time jobs he has held so far.

> *8 March 2004 – Just several days ago, talking about the issue of me seeking a job, I had a disagreement with my parents when my mother said "Don't you have any interest in starting by stocking supermarket shelves, etc." and I flatly refused. Here's the reason I gave her: "If it is not connected to the next job, it won't count towards job experience." I have gone for interviews many times. While I have confidence in myself*

since I have been fully recognized by the companies where I have previously worked, this work experience is not acknowledged at all during interviews. I had to experience this many times and I could not help ending up thinking "Ah, I am nothing ..."

Besides, if one works for low wages without any motivation, surely one will increasingly lose self-respect and sad thoughts might lead to thoughts about suicide. Last night a SMAP song "The only flower in the world" (Was it that?), said "♪It is ok not to be number one since originally one is unique♪" This encouraging song became a hit, but in companies and organizations things are not like this. Even among freeter, there is competition and if results are bad, one will be fired. This is the truth.[123]

Thus this diary writer might well, and with good reasons on his side, be counted as part of a group of young people that are being described with the latest acronym to grace the discussion on Japanese labor, this time not created in Japan but taken from the UK – NEET: Young people who are "Not in Employment, Education or Training" and are often still living with their parents.

Non-regular employees reported in their diaries about the difficulties finding regular work and named three factors as being responsible for their problems: the non-recognition of experience acquired as non-regular employees, employees doubting their sincerity, and finally age. The importance of all three factors has also been established through surveys.

Writers are actually correct in their perception that many employers do not regard experience acquired in non-regular employment as a positive asset. In the Employment Management Survey carried out by the Ministry of Welfare (response 74.3%, 4,266 companies) the majority of companies answered that having been a *freeter* would not influence their judgment in any way. Yet, 30.3% answered that they regarded such experience as negative, while only 3.6% regarded it as positive. The few companies that regarded having worked as a *freeter* as positive pointed to the experience that people have gained in their past employment or certain technical skills and knowledge that they thus might possess.

The factors that led to a negative stance were more varied (Chart 6.1) and a difference existed between larger and smaller companies.

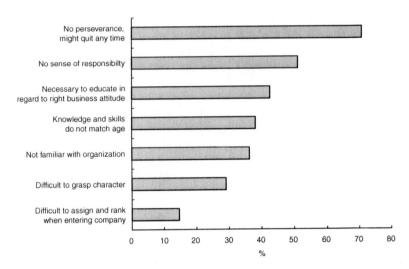

Chart 6.1 Reasons why companies take a negative view of employing *freeter* as regular employees (multiple answers in %)

Note: Employment management survey: only companies that viewed *freeter* experience as negative.

Source: MHLW 2004.

While smaller companies were mostly concerned about a lack of determination, perseverance and sense of responsibility of people who had been *freeter* in the past, larger companies were somewhat more concerned with organizational issues such as how to rank a person within the hierarchy or whether qualifications and age would match; strong signs that aspects of seniority are still of importance.

The results above run somewhat parallel to the general discussion on lifelong employment and changing jobs in Japan and can also be interpreted in this way. Besides strong reservations about perceived character flaws of *freeter,* companies also find it difficult to integrate *freeter* into their hierarchies because of age differences. The Employment Management Survey thus asked for the age at which companies would hire a *freeter* as a regular employee. In response 21.5% of corporations reported a very low acceptable age range of between 20 and 24 years; 26.0% would still hire people between 25 and 29 years; and 5% people between 30 and 34 years. However, 33.7% of corporations stated that they would hire people above 35 years of age. Due to all these factors the percentage of businesses that have actually employed a *freeter* stood at only 11.8% (MHLW 2004).

Age reservations might eventually become the most pressing topic for Japanese policy makers. Chart 6.2 shows that the average age of *freeter* is increasing and age restrictions by companies might already stand in the way of entry into regular employment for a large number of those employees.

However, it might be dispatch workers who could be hit most severely by age restrictions. Statistics show dispatch workers to be still relatively young, with many still only in their first positions. Yet, Weathers (2001) found that many client companies imposed age restrictions on female employees supplied to them by temporary staffing agencies. With advancing age, people seeking dispatch work might therefore be no longer referable by their agencies. Also, having exceeded the age that allows for entry into regular employment, older people might be forced into other non-regular employment types that offer much reduced levels of satisfaction in terms of work content and levels of pay. Yet, the indirect nature of employment

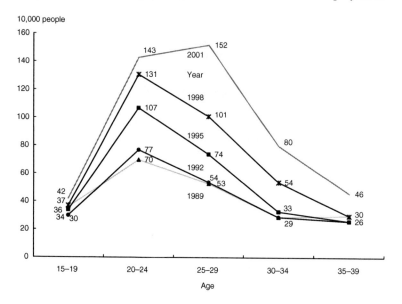

Chart 6.2   Change in composition of *freeter* population by age group (1989–2001)
Note: Based on Labor Force Survey.
Source: Naikakufu 2003.

through agencies stands in the way of effective countermeasures by policymakers to improve this situation.

Thus the question remains of whether it is possible to build a career in non-regular employment, possibly within the internal labor market of companies. Chapter 2 outlined how some employers have offered part-time employees the chance to advance or even to change their employment status to regular employment. Blog writers have also written about cases where non-regular employees perform more sophisticated tasks.

One of the blog writers had noticed the existence of team leaders among *freeter* who play a central role in the production process. This situation also caught the attention of researchers and was one of the central themes in the research project on subcontracting led by University of Tokyo researchers (Sato, Sano and Kimura 2003). The survey found that leaders were indeed largely recruited from non-regular employees. 30.5% of so-called leaders stated that they wanted to work as regular employees but could not do so, and another 16.1% stated that they entered with the intention of doing this work only until they could find a position as a regular employee.

While the emergence of team-leaders among non-regular employees might be seen as a positive sign, this picture is somewhat qualified when looking at the anxieties of team-leaders concerning their employment. Despite having achieved advancement to leader status, leaders still show nearly the same levels of anxiety concerning the security of their jobs, with the added factor that they feel the responsibilities they have to take on sometimes go beyond what is justified by their qualifications and position in the company.

The Japanese Institute of Labor Policy and Training reports a number of cases where people managed to advance from non-regular positions. Often in a franchise setting people managed to advance from *"arubaito"* to the position of store manager or even store owner; however the number of such cases still seems to be relatively small (JILPT 2004c). Gaston and Kishi (2007) also found evidence that part-time workers are screened by companies for regular employment. Yet, a survey by the government-affiliated Japan Institute of Worker's Evolution (21 Seiki Shokugyō Zaidan 2002) of 1,435 establishments found that many companies still did not have a proper system for career advancement of non-regular employees. 31.0% of workplaces did not differentiate part-timer remuneration at all, and 37.8% left the decision to differentiate wages at the discretion of branch managers. Only 27.5% had a system that included systematic increases in pay for part-timers. 62.7% had no system that allowed part-timers to change to regular employment, and even among the establishments that had such a system, 20% had not made use of it during the previous year. Equally 84.8% had no system that saw the advancement from part-timers to group leaders and even from the 11.3% of companies that had such a system only 63.4% had put it into real use. Finally, a survey by JILPT showed a major difference concerning the training of employees, with regular employees still undertaking training much more regularly (Chart 6.3).

Honda (2004) thus voiced serious doubts about whether equal treatment of part-timers and regular employees could really be achieved. Especially concerning remuneration he re-emphasized that non-regular employees were mainly employed because of lower labor costs; flexibility aspects were only of secondary importance. It thereby remains to be seen whether companies will be able to reconcile other objectives, such as having non-regular employees perform more responsible tasks, with their cost-saving objectives in

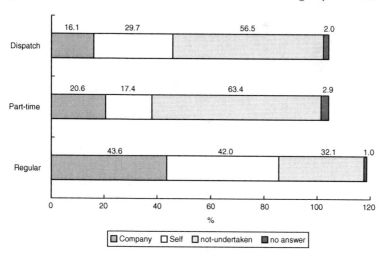

Chart 6.3   Skill development by employment type (in %)
Note: Multiple answers to question: have you undertaken training within the last year?
Source: JILPT 2004b: 312.

the long run. Consequently, Honda demanded major reforms not just in the management of non-regular employees but in the whole personnel management system of companies.

6.3   Situating non-regular employment

Many of the patterns of the Japanese employment system which have come to be considered as traditional are actually of fairly recent origin. For example, Yuki Honda (2004) argued that before the 1960s companies hired blue collar employees, who at that time far outnumbered white-collar employees, according to their short-term needs throughout the year. Companies only switched to a more systematic approach of hiring employees directly from school and at a certain point of the year when facing a labor shortage during the high-growth period. Equally Ogura (2005) argued that fixed-term contracts and indirect employment were the norm in Japanese manufacturing before legislation and labor shortages changed this situation, with permanent and direct employment becoming the norm. *"Historically speaking 'typical employment' (i.e. long-term stable employment) – the opposite of what is known as 'atypical employment' today – is a relatively new concept"* (Ogura 2005: 9).

Japan's situation in terms of non-regular employment is not unique, and in most major countries so-called non-regular, non-standard or atypical forms of employment have gained in importance (Kalleberg 2000). At the same time, significant changes have occurred concerning the characteristics of this employment type. Kalleberg argues that:

> *Part-time work in the United States and other countries (such as Japan – ...) in recent years has thus changed from an activity that mainly accommodates the needs of the workforce for shorter hours to one that meets employers' needs and preferences for such things as lower costs and more flexible staffing.*

Indeed, Kalleberg's statement captures the essence of what is currently happening in Japan. Companies have been increasing the number of non-regular employees, and blog writers' accounts as well as surveys have shown that non-regular employees have become an indispensable part of the Japanese workforce. At the same time, motives for employees to take up non-regular employment have become more varied. A significant number of people take up non-regular employment because they have no other alternative, while others do not like the restrictions that go along with being regularly employed and thus take it up as an alternative to regular employment.

Concerning non-regular employment the so-called *freeter* phenomena needs further discussion. Again, while Japan has provided us with a nice new term, the phenomenon itself is not exclusive to Japan. Gorz argues that:

> *The fact needs to be publicly and widely recognized that, dependent employment as well as secure full-time workplaces are not the social normality. Rather, the forming actors of this new normality are all those employed precariously, those who work sometimes and sometimes not, who change between several jobs, of which none is accepted nor a real calling, whose job it is to have none, who consequently cannot and do not want to identify with their work and who bring all their energy into their "real" occupation that they perform when they are not working.* (Gorz 2000: 77)

He continues:

> *Generation X, by refusing to bind itself through full-time employment and long-term to a company, defines itself not through its workplace. Its representatives have a personal plan that counts more than the objectives of an organization they work for and that motivates them more through concern about ethical values and social responsibility then work ethics.* (Gorz 2000: 87)

Gorz relates this situation not only to developments on the demand side but also holds companies responsible who by no longer offering permanent employment have become pure job providers, and as such are no longer regarded as family. Gorz thereby assumes a general world-wide reduction in the importance that employees attribute to their work.

While this might be true for some, the blog excerpts in this book show that people still consider their own work to be of major importance. In workplaces, co-workers form relationships with each other, even if some might initially feel that they do not want to do so, and even non-regular employees spend a significant amount of time thinking about their work.

The diary entries and surveys also show that the situation of most Japanese non-regular employees is certainly not as positive and glamorous as outlined by Gorz for his generation X. Indeed, some commentators in Japan argue that a group of young people has developed that has lost their aspirations and hope about their future. The discourse on this issue was initiated by a book by Masahiro Yamada, a professor at Tokyo Gakugei University and a popular social commentator. In his book *Expectation Gap Society* (*Kibō kakusa shakai*) (Yamada 2004) he argues that while society, education, school and employment have provided aspirations for young people in the past, this is increasingly no longer true for a large number of people. Therefore a gap develops between young people who still have aspirations in life and those who have not. His ideas spread quickly and in June 2005 a group of professors from the Institute of Social Sciences of the University of Tokyo came up with a "Declaration of Hopology" with the aim of studying hope in society systematically from the perspective of the social sciences.

The phenomenon of young people taking up or ending up in non-regular employment is also related to changing patterns in the transition from school and university to work. Looking at this development shows that it is a combination of a change in institutional relationships between schools and employers, the motivation of young people, and underdeveloped systems for the development of widely recognized skills and qualifications that largely feeds the pool of young people taking up or having to take up non-regular employment. In the past, the transfer from work to school was relatively well structured, and young people looking for their first regular jobs received much guidance. Under what can be called a periodical blanket hiring system, companies hired employees directly from school or university in a standardized manner at a certain point of the year and in close collaboration with schools or universities. However, Yuki Honda (2004) sees clear symptoms of a collapse of this system with a decreasing demand from firms for regular employees, firms diversifying their hiring practices, the collaboration between schools and employers deteriorating, and finally, younger employees having a high propensity to quit early in their first employment contracts.

> *In Japan today, the objective is to reorganize the transition from school to work into the form of a free marketplace, in which "able and vital" individuals can directly confront employers – who are no longer as generous and benevolent to young workers as they were in the past – without the former, strongly paternalistic intermediation of schools.* (Honda 2004: 113)

Honda sees some directions for the development of a new system; mainly more freedom for high-school graduates to choose their employers (in the past, under strict guidance from schools, high-school students were only allowed to apply to one employer at a time), the introduction of internships or trial employment, and finally measures to increase employability through skill development. Still, she is not very optimistic in regard to the future:

> *What is of greatest concern, however, is the enormous gap between the reality and the objective. Most Japanese youth have neither reliable vocational qualifications nor career designs, and are far from being "able and vital." Neither the quantity and quality of opportunities of continuing skills development and adult higher education can be compared to those in the US, despite the recent steady increase.* (Honda 2004: 113)

One of the worries concerning the increasing number of people in non-regular employment is the possibility of non-regular employment becoming the permanent state of employment for many of them. Until fairly recently most non-regular employees in Japan were provided with additional income or social security through other sources. For married women re-entering the workforce as part-timers this extra support came from husbands working as regular employees; for older employees it came from retirement allowances, pensions and assets accumulated during their working lives. Many students were working on the side while receiving support from their parents, and always with the promise of eventually becoming regular employees after graduation from school or university (Weathers in Satō, Osawa and Weathers 2001).

In contrast, many employees working in the new forms of non-regular employment, such as dispatch workers or employees of the on-site contractors sector, either by choice or necessity, do not have this kind of security. This is further aggravated through the introduction of intermediaries into the employment process. When no longer able to meet employers' requirements, these people have no recourse at the place where they work since they are employed through intermediaries. Here, especially the age bias of many Japanese corporations needs to be mentioned. It needs to be seen whether this will change with Japan's population ageing and the supply of younger people getting thinner. While dispatch work might appeal to many initially as a good alternative to either the rigid working conditions of regular employees or low paid employment as a part-timer, it has been shown that there is a danger of employees having to take up non-regular employment of lesser and lesser quality with advancing age.

The question of intermediaries is also important when looking at gender issues. Weathers (2005) argued that discrimination in Japan has increasingly taken indirect forms and that indirect discrimination has largely replaced the issue of direct discrimination in companies. Previously it was mainly the practice of companies to put male and female employees on different career tracks from the beginning that drew criticism. However, companies tend to avoid the gender issues of the past by outsourcing the supply and administration of employees of certain occupations to temporary staffing agencies. Weathers claims that the regulations concerning non-regular work are largely inefficient and thus it is very difficult for women who feel unfairly treated to get their interests represented.

While it has often been argued that it is necessary to improve the treatment of non-regular employees to the same level of regular employees, the author of the final diary entry in this chapter shows another possible development path.

11 August 2003 – By the way, in our company, the designation into "regular employees" and "part-timers" has been done away with and changed to "general" and "regional." Then in the personnel system reform, "housing allowance" and the "family allowance" and other benefits on which regular employees have existed have been eliminated. Things are changing step by step. It now seems a dream that previously, even things such as lunch were paid for. In the short two years that I have been in charge of financing, the total payment to full-time employees has decreased through reductions in individual pay, reductions in the number of employees, and the shrinking of the company to a level of 60% of the original size. There seems no hope from now on.[124]

A survey by the Tokyo Chamber of Commerce (May 2002, 334 responses, 23.2%) shows that the majority of companies have recognized the need for equal treatment, and to reach this situation also believe that changes to the way that regular employees are treated are necessary. Regarding the groups for which change is required, 42.8% believe it is necessary for both groups, 14.7% just for regular employees and 6.9% only for the treatment of non-regular employees. Still it needs to be pointed out that with 30.8%, the share of companies that do not regard equal treatment as necessary at all remained high (Tōkyō Shōkō Kaigishō 2002).

Indeed, University of Tokyo professors Sato and Sano (2005) argue, based on a number of case studies on the management of non-regular employees, that it is necessary for companies to do away with the separation between non-regular employees and regular employees, and instead of the current diffuse situation, come up with employment categories that genuinely relate to job content and career development possibilities. They criticize that for many companies the employment type is still predetermined at the start of the hiring process, and only thereafter are other decisions made, such as those regarding work content, working hours, or length of employment. They also point out that many non-regular employees, through the continuous renewal of their contracts, have, at least in the view of the law, become permanent employees already, an additional reason for doing away with the regular/non-regular classification. If companies do not change their ways, Sato and Sano see the possibility of serious problems in terms of employee satisfaction, with consequences for productivity and the quality of goods and services. Earlier Sato had argued that:

> *in seeking balance of treatment between regular and non-regular employees, diversification of employment categories is essential. One hopes to see the day when one can work limited hours and still be a regular employee. Clearly, we need major changes in the treatment of*

regular employees as well as non-regulars, and this in turn necessitates a fundamental rethink of the rules of employment and dismissal. (Satō in *Satō, Osawa and Weathers* 2001: 219–220)

In summary, while some initiatives exist to help non-regular employees build careers and to improve their long-term options, the current situation for non-regular employees does not look very promising. While Capelli's proposal of the resurgence of the "frightened worker" model as introduced in Chapter 2 might not yet apply to Japan's regular workers, it might well apply to many in Japan's growing non-regular workforce.

7
Conclusions – Importance of Perceptions, Employability and Directions of Change

14 April 2003 – One of my high school classmates came home and I met her for the first time in a year. She is about the only classmate from my high school days I am still in contact with – a precious friend. A lot has happened to her since she began work. Everyone is working hard. Overall, there are many among my friends who say "I don't expect to be with this company for long" and she is one of them. I strongly think that with the company side having done away with lifelong employment, the employed side has also largely changed its mindset....fooling, being fooled, mutual deception??[125]

Fooling, being fooled, mutual deception? Can this be the final, simple conclusion of this book about the future relationship between employees and companies in Japan? Surely not! Too many writers have shown in their diaries genuine concern about the situation of their companies, and many companies have realized that they need to put in a genuine effort to reconcile measures to increase competitiveness with measures to keep their employees loyal and motivated.

This book began with an overview of company initiatives to change the management of human resources. It has been shown how changes in the environment have forced companies to reduce the size of their workforces and to make changes to their human resources management.

With corporate restructuring efforts, changing principles of employment and remuneration, and qualitative and quantitative changes to the role of non-regularly employed people, significant developments have taken place in Japanese workplaces. It was shown that corporate restructuring efforts have not only had an effect on people who had to leave their companies, but also demonstrated to remaining employees the difficulties that Japanese corporations faced in following up on promises of lifelong employment. Changes in the principles of employment and remuneration have reduced the importance of age, family status or long-term efforts and instead promoted individual achievement. Finally, the increase in numbers of irregular employees and changes to the way they are utilized have challenged the position of regular employees.

The question is, how can these changes be related to each other? Are they reinforcing each other or are they contradictory? Are they driving the elements of the Japanese employment system in the same direction or are they pulling them apart?

In the following, the issues discussed in this book will be summarized into several main points. The first point to be taken up is the effects of the developments highlighted in this book on those elements of Japanese management that have been considered as defining Japanese corporations, such as the possibility of planning long-term, team work, quality control or continuous improvement. Secondly, developments will be put into an even wider context by looking at the significance of the described developments when related to the concept of employability and the development of external labor markets.

Chapter 1 referred to the earlier work of Pucik and Hatvany (1980) and Itoh (1994) who have described the management of human resources in Japan as being at the core of a highly integrated management system. The way human resources were managed was linked to a number of advantageous effects, such as the possibility for long-term corporate development, the continuous improvement of products and production processes, quality control and the ability to utilize tacit knowledge. Itami (1994) provides a further example of this line of thought by pointing to employee sovereignty as the main characteristic of the Japanese firm. He admits that this is limited to the group of core employees and excludes part-time and female workers, but still, for the group of core employees, the feeling of ownership and sovereignty leads to a strong identification with the firm that goes far beyond providing labor on a purely contractual basis. Within this

[handwritten annotations in margin]

setting it was then rational for employees not to look for short-term advantages, but to take a long-term view and behave accordingly. Consequently, information sharing was encouraged, knowledge was widely distributed and decision making became more efficient, and in addition, stratification tendencies in workplaces were countered. People could work relatively effectively in teams and did not have to think about individual advantages in terms of accumulation of knowledge or skills since much of the technical knowledge was actually held by shop-floor workers.

Finally, Itami consolidated the various elements of his argument by describing Japanese firms as being held together by a well-balanced system of sharing:

> *If one person receives relatively more money and another relatively more substantial power in decision making, each can have his or her own source of satisfaction, and a sense of fairness prevails. Social harmony in the workplace is more easily attained than if a limited number of people monopolize all three – money, authority, and information.*
> (Itami 1994: 85)

[handwritten annotation: Japanese firm as a community]

While not everybody entirely agrees with Itami's views of the nature of the Japanese firm (for example Tabata [1998] describes the Japanese firm as a community that is largely held together by market pressures and the lack of external labor markets), the developments described in this book have clear implications for the running of the Japanese firm.

Itami's first point, the identification of employees with the firm and the existence of a core group of employees that develops a high sense of belonging to the firm through this status, is threatened by the fact that the core group in Japanese companies is shrinking as increasing numbers of non-regular employees are brought in. This often goes with the blurring of lines between regular and non-regular employees. At the same time, companies are emphasizing differences between regular employees more than in the past through the introduction of merit-based incentive systems. However, if companies distinguish very clearly between the role of regular and non-regular employees, companies might eventually find that the core group of loyal employees with a sense of belonging becomes too small to carry the full weight of the company.

[handwritten annotation: core group vs non reg employees challenge]

In his second point Itami argues that employees align their own interests with the long-term interests of corporations. Concerning the increasing number of non-regular employees it has been shown that many non-regular employees do not want to get involved in the long-term development of the company. Restructuring efforts by companies and changes in company relationships have led some regular employees to recognize that they might not be able to reap the fruits of long-term engagement, and such attitudes are supported by new incentive systems that seem to favor employees who pursue short-term gains.

The accumulation and sharing of information across all levels of the organization has been challenged by the outflow of personnel in the wake of restructuring. By using more and more non-regular employees who are not employed by the company directly and for the long term, companies have also been finding it increasingly difficult to preserve and develop the knowledge and skills that normally accumulate in corporations. Non-regular employees, normally paid by the hour, find little incentive to accumulate knowledge, work long hours and spend time on activities outside working hours to discuss improvements of products or processes.

Overall, the balance in the distribution of information, power, and money proposed by Itami as the binding mechanism of Japanese firms therefore seems to be seriously threatened. Control over information, power and money seems to be increasingly concentrated within a shrinking group of people, and even within this group interpersonal relationships seem to be more competitive than in the past. It has been argued that properly fulfilling expectations in terms of relationships has been a major source of work satisfaction for Japanese employees; however the current changes force employees to rethink their conduct.

Tabata argues similarly:

For the firm-community, this will mean a contraction of its domain of existence, a reduced number of male and regular workers in large firms. At the same time, the structure of firm-communities is becoming more competitive – at the expense of the egalitarianism that is essential to community in general. Moreover, increases in transfers or early retirement programs weaken the credibility of the protective function of community. Furthermore, gender bias in employment is being criticized *more and more vigorously. All these factors combine to weaken the system of the firm-community, as well as people's faith in it.* (Tabata 1998: 213)

Japanese companies seem to have recognized many of the above issues and are currently looking for ways to reconcile the different needs they have. Most companies have not come up with a consistent new model yet. Thus the durability and impact of the current initiatives needs to be discussed.

Holzhausen (2000) argued that many developments that received much attention in the media during the 1990s were not really new or radical when seen in a historical perspective.

the gradual shift of emphasis from seniority to ability, which started long before the 1990s – after the first oil crisis in fact – does not contradict this but indicates that the instruments to achieve this aim have been changed. An interpretation that sees this development as signifying fundamental change is arguably based on a false understanding of employment practices, since it ignores their evolution during the last 20 years. (Holzhausen 2000: 232)

Holzhausen's assessment may be partially due to the fact that developments gained in speed and depth only after the publication of his paper. Nevertheless, his statement raises an interesting point. When looking at the relationship between employees and employers, it is perceptions as well as the objective state of things that matter. Blog writers' experiences and opinions, as well as surveys, clearly show that employees do perceive the developments of the 1990s and later as fundamental changes. Indeed, it has been argued in Chapter 4 that it might be the heightened transparency and visibility of change that distinguishes the developments of the 1990s from earlier developments.

Debroux, however, has argued that the developments in the Japanese employment system are more than an issue of perception but are really leading to significant change.

New initiatives departing more distinctly from the traditional principles are taken, putting into question the relational psychological contract between employees and companies, i.e., the dominant work ideology.

> *The concept of the company as a community assuring the long-term employment and welfare of the regular employee is seriously challenged for the first time since the war. This time it is not only in terms of consciousness of the employees and a half-hearted wish for change from management but in terms of actual behaviour of the two parties.* (Debroux 2003: 17)

Indeed, while the significance of single developments and events has often been questioned, it might eventually be the aggregated results of various processes that give the developments since the 1990s a special importance. Perceptions of employees about their work and relationship with their employers are not the result of single observations but form over time and are based on a variety of experiences and observations. Not all changes in perceptions lead to immediate changes in behavior and actions; some might need certain events or certain changes in the environment to occur before they are translated into action.

In the following, this can be shown by taking up the issue of employability – an issue much discussed not only in Japan but in all highly developed economies. The lack of external employment markets has been described as a major characteristic of the Japanese employment system of the past. While a number of mutually reinforcing factors accounted for this situation, firm-specific training of employees and the resulting specificity of skills acquired were major factors that supported this state of development. At the same time, employees were viewed as generalists by their employers and as part of their firm's development process were frequently transferred across the various functions of the firm. Employees were left largely unaware of their own skills and abilities and many were therefore not able to sell their own "skills" to potential employers. Equally, firms found it difficult to evaluate the skills and experience of job candidates who wanted to make a mid-career change of employers.

The developments outlined in the previous chapters are all related to this point. While single factors might not be substantial enough to drive change, in combination they might lead to an increased employability of Japanese employees, with employees as well as employers becoming more aware of skills possessed as well as skills needed. At the same time, employers and employees might become more capable of communicating their needs and demands to each other. It has been argued in Chapter 3 that restructuring measures (especially early retirement exercises and changes in the transfer system) have forced Japanese employees to reconsider their own positions within and outside their companies. This has not been the case only for employees who left or were forced to leave their original employers, but also has become a necessity for employees who stayed behind.

Even though many employers still publicly emphasize their commitment to long-term employment, and probably also truly believe in the merits of this employment principle, it is questionable whether they will really be able to stand by their commitments. The possibility of direct transfers was an important element of the long-term employment system since it guaranteed employment to older workers and perhaps even more importantly, it made available positions of status that were appropriate to the age of older workers. However, the weakening of corporate groupings has made direct transfers between corporations more difficult and investors and regulators are increasingly calling for more transparent corporate relationships.

In summary, restructuring exercises forced many employees to think about the chances of employment outside their companies. However, searching for employment outside one's own company does raise the question of employability, and it was shown that many Japanese employees did not possess skills that were recognized outside their own workplaces, or were not aware of the skills they had, or were not able to present their skills adequately to potential new employers.

However, the introduction of results-based remuneration systems has the potential to change this situation to a certain degree. It has been shown that while many employees did not oppose the introduction of results-based remuneration systems from the outset, their opinions changed after they experienced major shortcomings in the way that systems were implemented. One of the shortcomings resulted from the point that fair evaluation of individual achievement required the sudden need to define work content precisely – a major undertaking in an environment that up to then had regarded people as team-oriented generalists. In their doubts about the introduction of the new principles of remuneration, employees were reassured by an overall very negative reaction in the media.

Companies, however, see no real alternative to the introduction of such merit-oriented systems. Therefore they will increasingly be

forced to come up with more precise job descriptions as well as standards by which performance can be measured. Accordingly, employees need to be given the possibility of developing skills in certain
areas, and increasingly demand to be allowed to develop skills that
are recognized not only in their own organization but across companies. An additional characteristic of the new evaluation systems is
that employees themselves are very much involved in the process of
defining objectives and also have to report their achievements regularly to superiors. In this process they not only develop awareness
of their own skills and value to the organization but also develop
the skills necessary to present themselves adequately to potential
employers outside the organization.

The quantitative and qualitative changes in the employment of
non-regular employees also have the potential to considerably change
the organization of work in Japanese firms. It has been shown that
major problems in the increased use of more non-regular workers ori-
ginate from the vague separation of tasks performed by non-regular
and regular employees. This situation is not necessarily due to a conscious policy by employers but might rather be due to the traditional
view that all employees working in the company are generalists.
However, this situation might affect the motivation of employees,
since they find themselves in a situation where monetary and non-
monetary incentives do not match initial expectations towards work
content. At the same time, regular employees feel threatened by non-
regular employees performing tasks similar to their own. The unclear
definition of tasks also leads to problems in the communication with
intermediaries such as temporary work agencies or sub-contractors
who provide on-site services. In addition, problems occur with regulators and other interest groups who increasingly see non-regular
employment as contributing to the indirect and hidden discrimination against certain groups of employees. So if companies want to
continue to enjoy the cost and flexibility advantages of employing
non-regular employees they will have to define tasks for regular as
well as non-regular employees more clearly than in the past.

Indeed, many companies are currently in the process of reorganizing tasks, and some companies have realized that the current significant differences in treatment based solely on the division of
non-regular and regular employment might stand in the way of
doing so properly and efficiently. Some companies have even gone

so far as to start introducing differences in pay and treatment based on different occupations from the beginning of employment.

Finally, politics, the bureaucracy, think tanks and academia have realized that there are potential problems concerning social security and stability that come with a large number of people working permanently in non-regular employment. So far, most companies have not been prepared to positively recognize the skills and experiences acquired through work in non-regular employment, and instead have assumed negative qualities in non-regular employees, such as shortcomings in regard to perseverance and commitment. Another problematic area is age. Currently most people working permanently as non-regular employees still fulfill the age requirements of employers since the increased popularity of on-site contracting or dispatch work is a relatively recent phenomenon. Eventually however, some people will fall out of the group of sought after people due to advancing age, and may be left with very few alternatives. Due to the use of intermediaries in the process of employing non-regular employees there is very little that regulators can do to counter this form of age discrimination directly. Lastly, the decreasing functioning of the system of university and school assisted job placements makes it more difficult for young people to find employment.

Consequently, the above interest groups call for the introduction of an education and training system that can equip people with generally recognized skills and qualifications and thereby ease the problems currently experienced in the labor market.

Nohara argued in 1999 that the many developments in the Japanese human resources management system cumulatively have the potential to lead to mobilization of actors and thereby to greater change.

Some of the institutional innovations constitute a direct assault on the most widely legitimated rules on which the Japanese model of HRM is based and are intended to create new patterns of behaviour among employees. Indeed, close observation of what is happening on the ground shows that the creation of new rules is being accompanied by innumerable attempts at mobilization involving the social partners or interactions between individual actors. In this sense, what might be called structural change already exists in an embryo-type form although, taken as a whole, the micro-innovations that are taking place are not

> *yet coming together to form a clearly-defined, coherent whole, in other words a new model of HRM.* (Nohara 1999: 260)

Since Nohara wrote his article, developments have certainly gained in pace but still no clear picture of a future management and employment system has emerged. Nevertheless, while none of the developments described in this book might be strong enough in isolation to change the state of Japanese labor markets, it has been shown how their combined materialization will have significant effects on employer-employee relationships in Japan. On the one hand, the position of employees might be strengthened by making it easier for employees to develop careers across different companies. On the other hand, however, employers might raise the demands they make of employees, and employees might find themselves in an increasingly competitive situation in their workplaces with the need to take much more care in planning not only their careers but their whole lives.

The data presented in this book has shown that employees have realized this situation and are split in their assessment of it. While some appreciate the new opportunities provided to them, others long for a return to a situation where it was mainly their employers that took care of their long-term security. However, this polarization is less than clear, with many employees being uncertain, clearly realizing the advantages and disadvantages of the old as well as the new systems.

It needs to be seen whether companies will find flexible ways to reconcile the two approaches or whether Japan is on the way to what Capelli (1999) has for the US described as the development of an independent market-driven workforce where both employees and employers largely seek short-term rewards, but do so under the assumption of a shared responsibility for guaranteeing the employability of employees.

In regard to the US, Capelli has also argued that increased self-responsibility in terms of the development of skills as well as career development leads to increased inequality between those who can provide for themselves and the many who cannot. Here, he especially points to the problems of younger employees in finding entry-level jobs that provide them with basic skills. Looking at the large number of younger people in non-regular employment in Japan, Capelli's conclusion again seems to fit the situation in Japan.

In summary, Japanese employees seem to experience in their work-places many of the developments that people in other countries have already experienced or are still experiencing. However, it might be too early to assert this with certainty. A number of questions can be outlined that must be considered again in the future. Among those questions are the following.

Can it be that the current period is just a transitional one that puts special strain on employees? This argument has been proposed to support the introduction of results-oriented remuneration systems. In the short run the introduction of results-oriented remuneration systems speeds up generational change and differentiates between employees, and might therefore be of importance in overcoming a situation of limited advancement opportunities and tight budgets. However, in the long run, such systems might lead to a situation where people are largely selected and remunerated based on their professional skills. Tabata (1998) also sees the possibility of corporate community bonds largely being replaced by professional bonds between contractual workers.

The argument of current changes marking just a possible transitional stage can also be brought forward for non-regular employment. The increase in numbers of non-regular employees and changes in the way they are utilized have put pressure on regular employees to accept changes in their own employment situation. However, at the same time, some companies are bringing employment conditions of non-regular employees closer to those of regular employees. Also, company unions, that have so far largely seen themselves as only representing the interests of regular employees, are increasingly realizing that they can only stay relevant if they start allowing non-regular employees into their ranks. Commentators in Japan are always creative with words and trying to identify new trends; there is already talk of regular-non-regular employees and non-regular-regular employees. Thus the increase in numbers of part-timers might just be a way to reinvent the Japanese employment system at lower cost and with regained elements of flexibility.

A major open question concerns the future demographic situation of Japan. Japan is a rapidly ageing society and it might soon be demographic changes that will dominate the discussion on the Japanese employment system. Another issue concerns the possibility of bringing more foreign workers into Japan. Already many employees in non-regular employment in manufacturing are non-Japanese workers, and the number of such workers is expected to increase in the future. In the long run, properly integrating these employees into Japanese workplaces is a significant challenge that might overshadow some of the other issues outlined in this book.

The final thoughts will, however, be about the phenomenon of diary writing on the Internet. I hope that by discussing the changes in Japanese workplaces this book has also shown the usefulness of Internet diaries or blogging to discuss and illustrate relatively recent developments in contemporary Japanese society and business. Since blogging is highly popular in Japan, and since blogs are easily accessible regardless of time and place, they are of special interest to the foreign researcher. Too often discourses are dominated by the views of Japanese policy makers, businesses or media, whose views are much easier to access. Turning this argument around, blogs might also be a way for Japanese policy makers, business leaders, the media and academics to stay in contact with the daily experiences, thoughts, perceptions and concerns of their own people. Therefore, it is hoped that diaries on the Internet will be more than just a fleeting fad or fashion.

The book began with a blog entry and therefore will also conclude with one. The first diary entry in this book was written by a diary writer whose company was still stuck in restructuring, leaving him in a situation where he was unsure about his future. The final diary entry is of quite a different nature. It asks people to make up their minds and simply forget about the period of the bubble economy and accept the current period of uncertainty and change as the norm. With economic recovery having been announced numerous times over the last decade but not having been fully realized, such a mindset would certainly serve the Japanese people. Still it is hoped that a model of work and management will evolve in Japan that is not only competitive from an international perspective but that also allows employees to work according to their wishes and needs in a fair setting.

2 May 2004 – Children who were primary school students during the period when Japan made a great fuss about being "Trapped in recession!" will soon have grown up and will be looking for work. Rather than striving for a period with an economy as prosperous as before, calling for "revival" and "restoration," wouldn't it be much smarter to create the feeling that the present state is "normal" and from there on work hard to move upwards. I think it is a problem of perception. Isn't it mentally exhausting to cry "my current position is lower than previously," "I need to return to the previous place." I think it is more important to look ahead saying "let's go there," and create a forward-looking spirit. This may be difficult for people who worked for companies during the period of the so-called bubble economy. However, if one does not know about this period, young people who have just entered society will surely be able to think this way.[126]

Notes

1. Male, http://wing.zero.ad.jp/~zbk33441/diary/diary_2001_06.html
2. Shin risutora nikki, http://blog.livedoor.jp/shopgirlblog/
3. Male, http://www3.diary.ne.jp/user/305432/
4. Male, http://www.geocities.com/Tokyo/7039/diary9910.htm
5. No information, http:/www.2.diary.ne.jp/user/60732
6. Male, http://www.hpmix.com/home/kenkenya/OLD/D3_4.htm#112
7. Male, http://diary.note.ne.jp/28192/
8. 50-year-old housewife, http://carsalonmori.cool.ne.jp/ranran/nikki_22. htm
9. Male engineer in late 30s, http://www.d6.dion.ne.jp/~endoumso/ diary5–4.htm
10. About 50-year-old male, link withheld as requested by author
11. About 50-year-old male, link withheld as requested by author
12. No information, http://village.infoweb.ne.jp/~truelove/diary/n0004.html
13. Male, assistant manager, http://www2.diary.ne.jp/user/112009/
14. 42-year-old male, computer-related work, http://www10.cds.ne.jp/~fryhsuzk/ bywriter.html
15. 39-year-old male office worker, http://www.h3.dion.ne.jp/~blue_is/ link41.htm
16. Older male employee of chip manufacturer, http://www.ctb.ne.jp/~fumio/ diary.html
17. Younger female office worker, http://lion.zero.ad.jp/k-agata/200002.htm
18. No information http://www.asahi-net.or.jp/~XW8T-YMSK/Others/ Diary/2002/0206.html
19. Business man in 20s, http://www.pluto.dti.ne.jp/~yurica/iitai/0111.html
20. 39-year-old male, formerly employed in subsidiary of large electronics manufacturer, now employed in family business, http://www1.plala.or. jp/maria/diary4.htm
21. Male, link withheld as requested by author
22. Male office worker, http://www2.mnx.jp/~jaj4921/2002–5.html
23. 40-year-old male employee in finance industry, http://village.infoweb. ne.jp/~fwkb5565/nikki6.htm
24. 32-year-old male employee in software development, http://www. tomyzoo.com/diary/old/200204.html
25. 30-year-old female employee, http://www2s.biglobe.ne.jp/~uyouyo/ diary/diary2000/diary00013.html
26. 43-year-old male employee, http://www.neversite.com/home/tsubat- suba/nikki/200204.html
27. Female writer of computer manuals, http://www.princess.ne.jp/~mew/ diary/diary02/200203b.html

28. Male, http://village.infoweb.ne.jp/~fwie8707/sub6–0204.htm
29. Male, http://dac.lolipop.jp/diary/200203.html
30. 30-year-old female employee, http://www2s.biglobe.ne.jp/~uyouyo/diary/diary2000/diary00013.html
31. Male, http://wing.zero.ad.jp/~zbk33441/diary/diary_2001_06.html
32. 52-year-old male office worker, http://www1.plala.or.jp/kaokaokk/zakkann2000–08.htm
33. Male employee in his 30s, http://takzou.hp.infoseek.co.jp/diary/D0211.htm
34. Younger female employee, http://www.diary.ne.jp/user/51728/
35. Older male employee, http://taruiyes.hp.infoseek.co.jp/maestro/005020802.html
36. 41-year-old male employee, http://www33.tok2.com/home/yotandai/nikki2000nen1gatu.htm
37. 25-year-old male, employer, http://www2.diary.ne.jp/user/176426/
38. Female early 30s, http://www2.diary.ne.jp/user/168896/
39. 32-year-old male, http://www3.diary.ne.jp/user/345165/
40. Male, http://www.enpitu.ne.jp/usr7/71927/diary.html
41. Female, http://diarynote.jp/d/43028/_0_10.html
42. Female, http://nansyuu.hp.infoseek.co.jp/kokoku09.htm
43. 36-year-old male, digital creator, http://homepage2.nifty.com/popn/Geoid/Update_log05.htm
44. Middle-aged male, http://www4.diary.ne.jp/user/441324/
45. 39-year-old male? http://home.att.ne.jp/green/bebop-tp/opinion.htm
46. 23-year-old female office worker, http://www3.diary.ne.jp/user/326707/
47. 26-year-old male, http://www2.diary.ne.jp/user/82592/
48. 25-year-old female in export business, http://www2.diary.ne.jp/user/147899/
49. Female, http://diarynote.jp/d/48586/20040526.html
50. Male, http://www.diary.ne.jp/user/34864/
51. Male, http://diarynote.jp/d/18725/_0_340.html
52. Male, http://diarynote.jp/d/21337/20040329.html
53. Female, http://www3.diary.ne.jp/user/329880/
54. Female in her 20s, computer-related work, http://www3.diary.ne.jp/user/333611/
55. Mid 50s male, http://www.diary.ne.jp/user/46343/
56. Male office worker, http://www2.diary.ne.jp/user/159754/
57. Female, http://diarynote.jp/d/28742/_0_20.html
58. 28-year-old male engineer, http://www2.diary.ne.jp/user/164438/
59. Male system engineer, http://www3.diary.ne.jp/user/345829/
60. Male, http://diarynote.jp/d/18725/_0_460.html
61. Male, http://diarynote.jp/d/32563/20030904.html
62. Male, http://www3.diary.ne.jp/user/311752/
63. Male, http://www2.diary.ne.jp/user/94480/
64. Younger male employee, http://www.aga5.com/slot/diary/0209/04.html
65. 38-year-old male office worker, http://homepage1.nifty.com/tagu/essay2000.htm

66. Male, http://diarynote.jp/d/10584/20020918.html
67. Male, http://www2.diary.ne.jp/user/111091/
68. Male in his mid 20s, http://diary.note.ne.jp/d/11785/_0_20.html
69. 29-year-old, female, http://diary.note.ne.jp/d/17337/_0_330.html
70. 3-year-old, male, http://diary.note.ne.jp/d/18725/_0_600.html
71. Female, http://diary.note.ne.jp/d/28895/
72. Female medical clerk, http://www.diary.ne.jp/user/51980/
73. Female part-time worker in 30s, http:www2.diary.ne.jp/user/137187/
74. Same as previous footnote, www2.diary.ne.jp/user/137187/
75. 25-year-old female, http://www4.diary.ne.jp/user/415833/
76. Female, http://www2.diary.ne.jp/user/110867/
77. Male in his late 30s, *arubaito*, http://diarynote.jp/d/38791/
78. Student, male, http://diarynote.jp/d/46210/
79. 24-year-old male, http://diarynote.jp/d/26953/_0_50.html
80. Male, unemployed, studying for professional degree, http://diary.note.ne.jp/d/11785/_0_110.html
81. Male, http://diarynote.jp/d/37437/_0_50.html
82. 27-year-old female, http://www.diary.ne.jp/user/49357/
83. Female, http://diarynote.jp/user/19310/
84. Female, http://www2.diary.ne.jp/user/92623/
85. Female, http://diarynote.jp/d/29082/20040114.html
86. Female dispatch worker, http://www2.diary.ne.jp/user/90147/
87. Younger female, http://www.diary.ne.jp/user/18796/
88. Younger female self-employed contractor, http://diarynote.jp/d/42415/_0_110.html
89. Male, http://diarynote.jp/d/12502/_0_370.html
90. Female, http://diarynote.jp/d/26872/_0_350.html
91. Female employee for subcontractor, link withheld as requested by author
92. Female, http://diarynote.jp/d/32748/_0_130.html
93. Male worker for on-site contractor, http://diarynote.jp/d/21337/_0_280.html
94. 33-year-old worker, http://www2.diary.ne.jp/user/166669
95. Female, http://diary.note.ne.jp/d/36810/_0_110.html
96. Male?, *freeta* in high tech industry, http://www4.diary.ne.jp/user/414935/
97. Male *arubaito*, link withheld as requested by author
98. 22-year-old male retail store manager, http://www3.diary.ne.jp/user/319544/
99. 22-year-old male retail store manager, http://www3.diary.ne.jp/user/319544/
100. Female dispatch factory worker, http://diarynote.jp/d/35724/_0_90.html
101. Female dispatch worker, http://diarynote.jp/d/11013/
102. Female dispatch worker, http://diarynote.jp/d/39701/_0_20.html
103. Female dispatch worker, http://diarynote.jp/d/25875/

104. Female contract employee, http://diarynote.jp/d/54981
105. Female part-timer, http://diarynote.jp/d/33616/_0_10.html
106. Male call center employee, http://www2.diary.ne.jp/user/106311/
107. Male contract employee, http://www.diary.ne.jp/user/46855/
108. Female contract employee early 30s, http://www.diary.ne.jp/logdisp.cgi?user=32018&log=200402
109. Male supervisor, http://diarynote.jp/d/33763/
110. Male administrative worker, http://diarynote.jp/d/38288/
111. 30-year-old male engineer, http://diary.note.ne.jp/d/19136/_0_330.html
112. Female, http://diarynote.jp/d/13307/
113. Male, http://diarynote.jp/d/46175/20040703.html
114. Female dispatch assistant sales person, http://diarynote.jp/d/34740/_0_60.html
115. Female, http://diary.note.ne.jp/d/23544/_0_100.html
116. Female, http://diarynote.jp/d/19671/
117. Younger female 'freeter', http://www2.diary.ne.jp/user/56809/
118. Female, http://diarynote.jp/d/37099/
119. Female, link withheld as requested by author
120. 35-year-old female temp staff, http://www.diary.ne.jp/user/40821/
121. 20-year-old female 'freeter', http://www2.diary.ne.jp/user/53874/
122. Female dispatch worker, http://diarynote.jp/d/11013/
123. Younger male 'freeter', http://diary.note.ne.jp/d/18725/_203.html
124. 32-year-old male, http://www2.diary.ne.jp/user/55339/
125. 26-year-old young mother, http://diarynote.jp/d/17015/_0_10.html
126. Female, http://diarynote.jp/d/33654/

References

Newspapers

NKS = Nihon Keizai Shinbun
NKS-NNI = Nihon Keizai Shinbun – Nikkei Net Interactive
NSS = Nikkei Sangyō Shinbun
NRSMJ = Nikkei Ryūtsū Shinbun MJ

21 Seiki Shokugyō Zaidan (2002) Tayō na shūgyō keitai no arikata ni kan suru chōsa kekka ni tsuite [Survey results concerning the diversification of employment patterns], Rōdō Taimsu, no. 816, April, pp. 5–32.

Appelbaum, Steven, Tamara G. Close and Sandy Klasa (1999) Downsizing, an examination of some successes and more failures, Management Decision, vol. 37, no. 5, pp. 424–436.

Broadbent, Kaye (2001) Shortchanged? Part-time workers in Japan, Japanese Studies, vol. 21, no. 3, pp. 293–304.

Brockner, Joel, Seven Grover, Thomas F. Reed and Rocki Lee Dewitt (1992) Layoffs, job insecurity, and survivors' work effort: Evidence of an inverted U-relationship, Academy of Management Review, vol. 35, no. 2, pp. 411–425.

Capelli, Peter (1999) The New Deal at Work, Managing the Market-Driven Workforce, Boston, Mass.: Harvard Business School Press.

Capelli, Peter, Laurie Bassi, Harry Katz, David Knoke, Paul Osterman and Micheal Useem (1997) Change at Work, New York, Oxford: Oxford University Press.

Cascio, Wayne F. (1993) Downsizing: what do we know? What have we learned? Academy of Management Executive, vol. 7, no. 1, pp. 95–104.

Choy, Jon (1999) Japan's Banking Industry: The 'Convoy' Disperses in Stormy Seas, Japan Economic Institute Report, no. 10, March 12, Tokyo: Japan Economic Institute.

Dawson, John and Roy Larke (2004) Japanese retailing through the 1990s: Retailer performance in a decade of slow growth, British Journal of Management, vol. 15, no. 1, pp. 73–94.

Debroux, Philippe (2003) Human Resource Management in Japan: Changes and Uncertainties, Aldershot, Hants: Ashgate.

Denki Rengō – Denki Sōken (2004) Denki sangyō ni okeru gyōmu ukeoi tekiseika to kaisei hakenhō e no taiō no kadai [Issues concerning the rectification of the situation in onsite contracting in the electronics industry and responses to changes in the dispatch law], Denki Sōken kenkyū hōkoku shiriizu, no. 7, Tokyo: Denki Rengō.

Dirks, Daniel (1999) Limits and latitudes of labour adjustment strategies in Japanese companies, in Japanese Management in the Low Growth Era, Daniel Dirks, Jean-Francois Huchet and Thierry Ribault (eds), Berlin: Springer, pp. 267–294.

EIRD-DBJ (Economic and Industrial Research Department Development Bank of Japan) (2002) *Prospects and Challenges Surrounding Japan's Electrical Equipment Industry: General Electrical Equipment Manufacturers' Restructuring of Operations and Future Prospects*, Development Bank of Japan Research Report no. 34, November 2004, Tokyo: Development Bank of Japan.

Fujimoto, Makoto and Tamura Kimura (2005) Business strategy and human resource management at contract companies in the manufacturing sector, *Japan Labor Review*, vol. 2, no. 2, pp. 104–122.

Furugōri, Tomoko (1997) *Hiseiki rōdō no keizai bunseki* [Economic Analysis of irregular labour], Tokyo: Tōyō Keizai Shinpōsha.

Gaston, Noel and Tomoko Kishi (2007) Part-time workers doing full-time work in Japan, *Journal of the Japanese and International Economies*, vol. 21, no. 4, pp. 435–454.

Genda, Yuji (2001) The unhappiness of middle-aged and older workers, *Japan Labor Bulletin*, vol. 40, no. 5, pp. 6-10, available at http://www.jil.go.jp/bulletin/year /2001/vol40–05/05.htm.

Genda, Yuji (2002) *Risutora chūkōnen no yukue* [The life of middle-aged employees after restructuring], ESRI Discussion Paper Series No. 10, Economic and Social Research Institute, Cabinet Office, Tokyo, Japan.

Genda, Yuji and Marcus E. Rebick (2000) Japanese Labour in the 1990s: Stability and stagnation, *Oxford Review of Economic Policy*, vol. 16, no. 2, pp. 85–102.

Gottfried, Heidi (2002) Commentaries 'atypical' and 'irregular labour' in contemporary Japan, *Social Science Japan Journal*, vol. 5, no. 2, pp. 245–248.

Grønning, Terje (1998) Whither the Japanese employment system? The position of the Japan Employers' Federation, *Industrial Relations Journal*, vol. 29, no. 4, pp. 295–303.

Hanami, Hiroaki and Saitō Tsuneaki (2004) Tokushū Nippon no genba ga abunai – monozukuri o mushibamu 'mitsu no trappu' [Special report: Production in Japan is in danger – the three snares that undermine the production of goods], *Nikkei Bijinesu*, 8 March 2004, no. 1232, pp. 30–45.

Holzhausen, Arne (2000) Japanese employment practices in transition: Promotion policy and compensation systems in the 1990s, *Social Science Japan Journal*, vol. 3, no. 2, pp. 221–235.

Honda, Kazunari (2004) *Shokuba no paato taimaa* [Part-time workers in the workplace], JILPT Rōdō seisaku repooto, no. 1, Tokyo: Rōdō Seisaku Kenkyū Kenshū Kikō.

Honda, Yuki (2004) The Formation and transformation of the Japanese system of transition from school to work, *Social Science Japan Journal*, vol. 7, no. 1, pp. 102–115.

Hoshi, Takeo and Anil Kashyap (1999) *The Japanese Banking Crisis: Where did it come from and how will it end?* NBER Working Paper 7250.

Inagami, T. and D. Hugh Whittaker (2005) *The New Community Firm: Employment, Governance and Management Reform in Japan*, Cambridge: Cambridge University Press.

Ishihara, Mamiko and Takehisa Shinozaki (2005) Why part-time workers do not accept a wage gap with regular workers, *Japan Labor Review*, vol. 2, no. 2, pp. 55–77.

Itami, Hiroyuki (1994) The 'Human-Capital-ism' of the Japanese firm as an integrated system, in *Business Enterprise in Japan: Views of Leading Japanese Economists*, Kenichi Imai and Ryutaro Komiya (eds), Cambridge Mass: MIT Press, pp. 73–88.

Itoh, Hideshi (1994) Japanese human resources management from the viewpoint of incentive theory, in *The Japanese Firm, The Sources of Competitive Strength*, Masahiko Aoki and Ronald Dore (eds), New York, Oxford: Oxford University Press, pp. 233–264.

JADA (Chūkō Nenreisha Koyō Fukushi Kyōkai) (2004) *Dai 11 kai kōreika shakai ni okeru kigyō to kōjin (jūgyōin) nen genkyō to taiō ni kan suru jittai chōsa* [11th survey concerning the situation of businesses and individual employees in the aging society], at: http://www.jada-prep.jp/research/home/2004.

JIL (Rōdō Kenkyū Kikō – Japanese Institute of Labor) (1999) *Shukkō * tenseki no jittai to tenbō* [Current situation and outlook on temporary and permanent inter-company transfers of personnel], Chōsa kenkyū hōkokusho, no. 126, Tokyo: Rōdō Kenkyū Kikō.

JIL (Rōdō Kenkyū Kikō – Japanese Institute of Labor) (2001) *Daitoshi no shūgyō kōdō to ishiki*, [Work conduct and work attitudes in large cities], Chōsa kenkyū hōkokusho, no. 146, Tokyo: Rōdō Kenkyū Kikō.

JIL (Rōdō Kenkyū Kikō – Japanese Institute of Labor) (2002) *Jigyō saikōchiku to koyō ni kan suru chōsa* [Survey concerning the re-organization of businesses and employment], (June), Tokyo: Rōdō Kenkyū Kikō.

JILPT (Japanese Institute of Labor Policy and Training) (2004a) *Labor Situation in Japan and Analysis 2004/2005*, Tokyo: Japanese Institute of Labor Policy and Training.

JILPT (Rōdō Seisaku Kenkyū Kenshū Kikō – Japanese Institute of Labor Policy and Training) (2004b) *Rōdōsha no hataraku iyoku to koyō kanri no arikata ni kan suru chōsa* [Survey concerning the inclination to work and employment management methods], JILPT chōsa shiriizu, no. 1, November, Tokyo: Rōdō Seisaku Kenkyū Kenshū Kikō.

JILPT (Rōdō Seisaku Kenkyū Kenshū Kikō – Japanese Institute of Labor Policy and Training) (2004c) *Kawaru kigyō shakai to korekara no kigyō*kojin*shakai no kadai* [Changing business society and companies, individuals and society of the future], Rōdō seisaku kenkyū hōkokusho no. L-3, Tokyo: Rōdō Seisaku Kenkyū Kenshū Kikō.

JILPT (Rōdō Seisaku Kenkyū Kenshū Kikō – Japanese Institute of Labor Policy and Training) (2005a) *Dai 4 kai kinrō seikatsu ni kan suru kekka sokuhō* [Preliminary result of the 4th survey concerning working life], 31 March, http://www.jil.go.jp/press/documents/20050331.pdf.

JILPT (Rōdō Seisaku Kenkyū Kenshū Kikō – Japanese Institute of Labor Policy and Training) (2005b) *Yuusufuru rōdō tōkei* [Useful Labor Statistics 2005], Tokyo: Rōdō Seisaku Kenkyū Kenshū Kikō.

JMA (Japan Management Association – Nihon Nōritsu Kyōkai) (2005a) *Seika shugi ni kan suru chōsa kekka no happyō* (Announcement of results of the survey concerning result-oriented principles), Press Announcement: 22 February, http://www.jma.or.jp/release/data/pdf/20050223.pdf.

JMA (Japan Management Association – Nihon Nōritsu Kyōkai) (2005b) *Seika shugi jinji ni kan suru kenkyū hōkokukai* [Meeting to report on the research concerning a merit-oriented human resources management system], http://www.jma.or.jp/keikakusin/2005/20050316_murahashi.pdf.

JPCSED (Japan Productivity Center for Socio Economic Development – Shakai Keizai Seisansei Honbu) (2004a) *Dai 7 kai Nihonteki jinji seido no henyō ni kan suru chōsa kekka gaiyō* [Overview of results of the 7th survey on changes in the Japanese personnel management system], 26 March.

JPCSED (Japan Productivity Center for Socio Economic Development – Shakai Keizai Seisansei Honbu) (2004b), *Heisei 16 nendo shin nyūshain (3842 nin) no 'hataraku koto no ishiki' chōsa kekka* [Results of the 2004 survey of 3842 newly recruited employees on 'work perceptions'], 17 June.

JPCSED (Japan Productivity Center for Socio Economic Development – Shakai Keizai Seisansei Honbu) (2005a) *Dai 8 kai Nihonteki jinji seido no henyō ni kan suru chōsa kekka gaiyō* [Overview of results of the 8th survey on changes in the Japanese personnel management system], 9 March.

Japanese Bankers Association (various years) *Zenkoku ginkō zaimu shōhyō bunseki* [Analysis of the balance sheets of banks], available at www.zenkinkyo.or.jp/stat/index.htm.

Joe, Shigeyuki (2004) *Uchigawa kara mita Fujitsu 'seika shugi' no hōkai* [The downfall of the performance-based pay system at Fujitsu as seen by an insider], Tokyo: Kobunsha.

Kalleberg, Arne L. (2000) Nonstandard employment relations: Part-time, temporary and contract work, *Annual Review of Sociology*, vol. 26, pp. 341–365.

Karake-Shalhoub, Zeinab A. (1999) *Organizational Downsizing, Discrimination and Corporate Social Responsibility*, Westport, Connecticut and London: Quorum Books.

Kato, Takao (2001) The end of lifetime employment in Japan? Evidence from national surveys and field research, *Journal of the Japanese and International Economics*, vol. 15, no. 4, pp. 489–514.

Kawaura, Yasuyuki (2000) Nikki komyunikeeshon [Communicating through diaries], *Gendai no esupuri*, 2000, no. 2, pp. 5–8.

Kawaura, Yatsuyuki, Yoshishiro Kawakami and Kiyomi Yamashita (1998) Keeping a diary in cyberspace, *Japanese Psychological Research*, vol. 40, no. 4, pp. 234–245.

Keene, Donald (1995) *Modern Japanese Diaries: The Japanese at Home and Abroad As Revealed Through Their Diaries*, New York: Henry Holt.

Keene, Donald (1999) *Travellers of a Hundred Ages – The Japanese as Revealed through 1,000 Years of Diaries*, New York: Columbia University Press.

Keizai Doyukai (2000) *Rōdō shijō no kakushin o mezashite* [Striving for a reform of the labor market], 14 June 2000, Tokyo: Keizai Doyukai.

Keizai Doyukai (2004) *Corporate Social Responsibility (CSR) in Japan*, CSR Survey 2003, Keizai Doyukai, January, Tokyo: Keizai Doyukai.

Keizai Sangyōshō (2004) *Dai 33 kai kaigai jigyō katsudō kihon chōsa kekka gaiyō* [Outline of the 33rd general survey on overseas activities], Tokyo: Keizai Sangyōshō.

Kōsei Rōdō Daijin Kanbō Tōkei Jōhōbu (2001) *Heisei 13 nen shūrō jōken sōgō chōsa kekka sokuhō* [Preliminary results of the general survey on the employment situation 2001], Tokyo: Kōsei Rōdōshō.

Kōsei Rōdōshō (2004) *Heisei 15 nen koyō kanri chōsa* [Employment management survey 2003], Kōsei Rōdōshō.

Kōsei Rōdōshō Kenkyū-kai (2001) Enpuroiabiritei handan kijun no sakutei o [About the setting up of standards for judging employability], *Nichirōken shiryō*, no. 1252, August, pp. 15–25.

Kōseirōdōshō (2003) *Heisei 15 nenpan rōdō keizei hakusho* [White paper on employment 2003], Tokyo: Nihon Rōdō Kenkyū Kikō.

Kosugi, Reiko (2004) 'Furiitaa' to wa dare na no ka [Who is a freeter?], *Nihon rōdō kenkyū zasshi*, April, no. 525, pp. 46–49.

KSS/KRS/MKS (Keizai Sangyōshō, Kōsei Rōdōshō, Monbu Kakagushō) (2003) *Heisei 5 Seizō kiban hakusho* [White paper on the foundations for manufacturing industries 2003].

KSS/KRS/MKS (Keizai Sangyōshō, Kōsei Rōdōshō, Monbu Kakagushō) (2004) *Heisei 16 Seizō kiban hakusho* [White paper on the foundations for manufacturing industries 2004].

Kuroda, Kenichi (2006) Japanese personnel management and flexibility today, *Asian Business & Management*, vol. 5, no. 4, pp. 453–468.

Kurosawa, Masako (2002) Manabi kōdō to shikaku katsuyō no jittai [Current situation of work conduct and use of qualifications], in Recruit Works Institute (Rikuruuto Waakusu Kenkyūjo) (ed.) *Koyō fuan to tenshoku no jittai – waakingu paason chōsa 2000 (bunseki hen)* [Current situation concerning employment insecurity and changing jobs, survey of working persons 2000, analysis volume], Tōkyō: Kabushikigaisha Rikuruuto, pp. 75–112.

Kuzmits, Frank E. and Lyle Sussman (1988) Early retirement or forced resignation: policy issues for downsizing human resources, *SAM Advanced Management Journal*, vol. 53, no. 1, pp. 28–32.

Leana, Carrie R. and Harry J. Van Burren III (2000) Eroding organizational social capital among US firms: The price of job instability, in *The Organization in Crisis*, Ronald J. Burke and Carry L. Cooper (eds), Oxford: Blackwell, pp. 221–232.

LeTendre, Gerald (1994) Guiding them on: Teaching, hierarchy, and social organization in Japanese middle schools, *Journal of Japanese Studies*, vol. 20, no. 1, pp. 37–51.

Lincoln, James R. and Yoshifumi Nakata (1997) The transformation of the Japanese employment system – nature, depth and origins, *Work and Occupations*, vol. 24, no. 1, pp. 33–55.

Littler, Craig R. (2000) Comparing the downsizing experience of three countries: a restructuring cycle? in *The Organization in Crisis*, Ronald J. Burke and Carry L. Cooper (eds), Oxford: Blackwell, pp. 58–77.

MHLW (Kōsei Rōdō Daijin Kanbō Seisaku Chōsabu – Sōgō Seisakuka) (2000) *Howaitokaraa o meguro saiyō no tayōka ni kan suru chōsa kenkyū hōkokusho*

[Report on the diversification of the employment of white-collar employees]. Tokyo: Kōsei Rōdōshō.

MHLW (Kōsei Rōdōshō) (2001) *Rōdōsha haken jigyō jittai chōsa kekka hokukosho* [Report on the results of the survey on the temporary staffing industry], Tokyo: Kōsei Rōdōshō.

MHLW (Kōsei Rōdōshō) (2004) *Heisei 16 nen koyō kanri chōsa kekka no gaikyō* [Outline of the results of the employment management survey 2004], Tokyo: Kōsei Rōdōshō.

MHLW (Kōsei Rōdōshō) (2007) *Haken rōdōsha ga tai zentoshi 26% sōka. 321 man nin* [Dispatch workers increase by 26% over the previous year to 3.21 million people], Kōsei Rōdōshō 28 December, http://www.mhlw.go.jp/houdou/2007/12/h1228–2.html.

Macromill Inc (2003) *Risutora ni kan suru ankeeto* [Research about restructuring], Risaachi no. 42036, http://www.macromill.com/client/r_data/category/index.html.

Mainichi Shinbun 19 March 2005, 06 nen shinsotsu saiyō [Employment of fresh graduates in 2006].

Mainichi Shinbun 13 April 2005, Keizai Sanshō: 'kakusa shakai' jidai no keizai unei saguru – iryō, kaigo, nenkin fuan kaishō [Economic Industrial Ministry: Probing into the running of the economy in the age of a 'differentiated society'. Erasing the uncertainties concerning medical services, nursing, pensions etc.].

Matanle, Peter C.D. (2003) *Japanese Capitalism and Modernity in a Global Era: Re-fabricating Lifetime Employment Relations*, London and New York: RoutledgeCurzon.

Matsushige, Hisakazu (2007) Employee comprehension of pay systems, *Japan Labor Review*, vol. 4, no. 2, pp. 104–120.

Meyer-Ohle, Hendrik (2003) *Innovation and Dynamics in Japanese Retailing*, Houndmills: Palgrave Macmillan.

Miyajima, Hideaki and Yishay Yafeh (2003) *Japan's Banking Crisis: Who has the Most to Lose?* Center for Economic Institutions Working Paper Series, CEI Working Paper Series, no. 2003–15.

Mizoue, Norifumi (2004) *Tonari no seika shugi* [The performance-based pay system next door], Tokyo: Kobunsha.

Morishima, Motohiro (2002) Pay practices in Japanese organizations: changes and non-changes, *Japan Labor Bulletin*, vol. 41, no. 4, pp. 8–13.

Morishima, Motohiro (2003) Changes in white-collar employment from the employee's perspective, *Japan Labor Bulletin*, vol. 42, no. 9, pp. 8–14.

Morishima, Motohiro and Tomoyuki Shimanuki (2005) Managing temporary workers in Japan, *Japan Labor Review*, vol. 2, no. 2, pp. 78–103.

NKS 1 July 2001, Hirogaru kigyō no seika shugi, kairyoku kuwaete made ima naze? [Spreading merit principle, why are companies speeding up their reforms now?].

NKS 25 August 2001, Kitakantō no chūkei shokuhin suupaa, komawari buki ni kentō [Medium-sized supermarkets in the eastern Kanto region, fighting bravely with fast revolving weapons].

NKS 29 August 2001, Surimuka isogu haiteku kigyō [High-tech businesses are speeding up the slimming of organizations].

NKS 22 September 2001, Shizugin, shinjinji seido ni raigetsu ikō – soshiki o furattoka [Shizuoka Bank switches to new personnel management system next month, flattening of hierarchies].

NKS 23 December 2001, Koyō dansō (1) Seishain zero kōjō [Employment dislocation (1) A factory with no regular employees].

NKS 22 February 2002, Matsushita akaji 4380 oku en, uriage daka genshō, kaikaku kōka sogu [Matshushita in the red with 438 billion yen, decrease in sales, revenues, results of restructuring offset].

NKS 17 March 2002, Toyota, bea zero no [Toyota stresses zero increase in basic pay].

NKS 4 April 2002, Saraba seishain keiei [Good-bye to regular employees in management].

NKS 1 May 2002, Ion seishain sayō tōketsu, rainen kara 2 nen, jinin 2 wari sakugen mokuhyō [Ion freezes new hiring or regular employees for 2 years from next year onwards, targets reduction of personnel by 20%].

NKS 24 May 2002, Dōgin, 3 nen de 500 nin sakugen [Personnel reduction of 500 people within three years].

NKS 8 July 2002, NECga sennin shain – seika shugi ni tomadoi ooku, hitsuyōna nōryoku wa? Noboshikata wa? [The full-time employees of NEC, many at loss concerning merit principle. What are the necessary abilities? How to grow?]

NKS 21 November 2002, Taishokukin wa jibun de kasage, kuzureru yokonarabi nōryoku jūki ni [Retirement allowance to be earned by oneself, crumbling uniform treatment, increasing importance of ability].

NKS 28 December 2002, Etsunen suru paato shogū rongi, seishain fukume seido saisekkei o [Withering theory on the use of part-timers, towards a system that includes regular employees].

NKS 7 March 2003, Asahigin, sōgō – ippan shoku kubun o haishi [Asahi Bank does away with separation between general and clerical track].

NKS 10 July 2003, Tottorigin, shokutaku, paato o kōin ni tōyō [Tottori Bank, contractual and part-time employees appointed as regular banking employees].

NKS 16 August 2003, 36sai no shitenchō, Mizuho ni tanjō, shanai kōbo de aki ni mo [A 36 year old branch manager has emerged at Mizuho, this year again internal advertising of positions].

NKS 17 November 2003, Teichaku ni wa kufū ga iru datsu nenkō gata chingin [A wage system that departs from seniority needs a framework to become established].

NKS 25 November 2003, Ginkō gyōkai ni seika shugi no nami, shiki kōjō hakaru [A wave of the introduction of merit based principles in the banking industry, aiming at an improvement of morale].

NKS 26 November 2003, Matsushita mo nenkō chingin haishi, raishun kara, zenshain taishō [Matsushita will abolish seniority wage, from next spring onwards, will affect all employees].

NKS 29 November 2003, Sonii wa 2004 nen 4 gatsu shoteate o senpai, kyūyo, kanzen seika shugi ni [Sony will totally do away with the various allowances, will move completely to merit-based principles].

NKS 16 January 2004, Sanyō, raishun ni mo shin seido, shinsotsu kara chingin kakusa, yūshū na jinzai o kōgū [Sanyo, from next spring onwards new system that includes wage differentials from fresh graduates onwards and preferential treatment for superior talent].

NKS 12 February 2004, Hyakkaten sabaibaru (shita) risutora kasoku [Survival of the department store (part 3), accelerating restructuring].

NKS 1 March 2004, Seizōgyō muke haken kaikin [Lifting of the ban on dispatch workers in manufacturing].

NKS 1 April 2004, Ukeoi rōdō, seizōgyō no kanshi kyōka [Contract workers, strengthening the monitoring in the manufacturing industry].

NKS 3 April 2004, Fueru saiyō [Increasing employment].

NKS 4 April 2004, Nyūkō 12 nenme no wakate mo, shitenchō ni sekkyoku kiyō [Young persons can become branch manager after only twelve years of joining the bank].

NKS 23 April 2004, Ōte suupaa, paato kumiai ni [Large supermarket chains let part-timers join unions].

NKS 13 May 2004, Jinzai haken ryōkin, jūyō kaifuku mo jōshōryoku wa nibuku [Fees for dispatch workers: even with a return in demand, upward trend is weak].

NKS 7 October 2004, Ōte suupaa shinsotsu saiyō semakimon, Seiyū, Yunii, raishun zero, Ion, Daiee, ōhaba gen ni [Large supermarkets only open a narrow gate for the employment of fresh graduates, Seiyu and Uny will hire zero, Aeon and Daiei will greatly reduce numbers].

NKS-NNI 8 April 2002, Hitachi gets 9000 applications for retirement program and NEC in 2002 recruited 5000 employees (*Nikkei Net Interactive* 5 August 2002) IT rebound: Chipmakers brace for tough times.

NKS-NNI 19 February 2004, Matsushita to abolish seniority-based promotions, appointments.

NKS-NNI 17 June 2005, Foreign ownership of 'Japan Inc' hits new high of 23.7%.

NSS 12 April 2002, Seika shugi chingin no kōsai, hirogaru seido minaoshi [Merrits and demerits of the merit principle, review of systems is spreading].

NSS 12 July 2002, Matsushita, kaden ōkoku no kunō, 'shea ubae' daigōrei [Matsushita, ordeal of the consumer electronics empire, snatching away of market share is the order of the day].

NSS 10 April 2003, Eigyō sutaffu ni paato josei kiyō, Saikyō Ginkō zen tenpo ni [Saikyo Bank to employ female part-timers as sales staff in all its branches].

NSS 27 May 2003, Taishoku kyūfu ni jitsuryokusei, Yokohama Ginkō, shiki kōshō nerau [Bank of Yokohama introduces merit-based system for retirement allowance, aiming at an improvement of morale].

NSS 2 April 2004, Gyomu ukeoi 100 man nin [1 million people in business subcontracting].

NSS 14 April 2004, Dai 1 bu V-kaifuku no danmen [Profile of the part V-shaped recovery].

Nagase, Nobuko 1995 *Joshi no shūgyō sentaku ni tsuite* [On women's employment choices], Doctoral dissertation, University of Tokyo.

Naikakufu (2003) *Heisei 15 nen kokumin seikatsu hakusho* [White paper on the national lifestyle 2003], Tokyo.

Nakakubo, Hiroya (2004) The 2003 Revision of the labor standards law: Fixed-term contracts, dismissals and discretionary-work schemes, *Japan Labor Review*, vol. 1, no. 2, pp. 4–25.

Nakata, Yoshifumi (1997) Nihon ni okeru danjo chingin kakusa no yōin bunseki: dō itsu shokushu ni tsuku danjo rōdōsha kan ni chingin kakusa wa sonzai suru no ka? [Analysis of factors in gendered wage differentials in Japan: Does a wage differential exist between male and female workers employed in the same occupational category?], in: *Koyō kankō no henka to josei rōdō* [Changing employment practices and female labour], ed. Chūma Hiroyuki and Suruga Terukazu. Tokyo: University of Tokyo Press, pp. 173–205.

Neumark, David (Ed.) (2000) *On the Job*, New York: Russel Sage Foundation.

Nihon Denki Kōgyōkai (2004) 2004 nendo denki kiki no seisan mitooshi [Outlook for the 2004 production of electronic machinery], *Denki*, no. 4, pp. 2–11.

Nihon Keizai Shinbun NNI 26 February 2004, Job & Wage: Merit-Based Pay Systems produce side-effects.

Nihon Kinyū Shinbun 20 December 2001, Kosuto asshuku, chigin mo kasoku – Shizuokagin, jinin sakugen, guruupu 500 nin, jingenhi 50 oku asshuku [Regional banks also accelerate the contraction of costs, Shizuoka bank reduces the number of group employees by 500 people, reduces costs by 5 billion yen].

Nihon Kinyū Shinbun 9 January 2003, Jūhachi Ginkō, ippan tenpo de hajimete no josei shitenchō tanjō [Juhachi Bank, emergence of first female branch managers in charge of normal branch].

Nihon Shōkengyō Kyōkai, (various years) *Tōkei jōhō* [Statistical information], www.jsda.or.jp/html/toukei/.

Nikkei Kinyū Shinbun 2 March 2001, Kansaigin 'kachō' haishi, guruupusei dōnyū [Kansai Bank – abolishment of section head, introduction of group system].

Nikkei Kinyū Shinbun 25 April 2002, Daishi Ginkō, jinjihi yokusei e shin-shokutaku seido [Daishi Bank, to suppress personnel costs, new commission system].

Nikkei Kinyū Shinbun 23 July 2002, Yokohama gin, jitsuryoku shugi o tettei, jinji seido sasshin, naibu kōbo o kakudai [Bank of Yokohama, thorough introduction of merit-based principles, reform of the personnel system, widening of internal advertising of positions].

Nikkei Kinyū Shinbun 25 August 2002, Gifugin, kōin 4 bun no 1 o idō, shinseido dōnyū [Gifu Bank transfers one quarter of its employees, introduces new system].

Nikkei Kinyū Shinbun 11 March 2003, Paato senryakuka e senmon soshiki, Hyakugogin, kakuten o junkan shidō [Hyakugo Bank sets up extra organizational unit to strategize use of part-timers, will rotate through branches and provide guidance].

Nikkei Kinyū Shinbun 10 September 2003, Marui, hankanhi, 200 oku en kyō o sakugen [Marui to reduce sales and administrative costs by 20 billion yen].

Nikkei Kinyū Shinbun 30 January 2004, Mitsubishi Shintaku, shingata keiei shūten ni josei no shōchō kiyō [Mitsubishi Trust and Banking Corporation will employ women in new business focus].

Nikkei Kinyū Shinbun 26 March 2004, Josei no shitenchō sekkyoku tōyō, Yokohamagin [Progressive emergence of female branch managers, Bank of Yokohama].

Nikkei MJ (Ryūtsū Shinbun) (2001) *Ryūtsū keizai no tebiki 2002* [Handbook of the distribution industry], Tokyo: Nihon Keizai Shinbunsha.

NRSMJ 29 February 2001, Shimamura jinji buchō Kubota Masatoshi [Shimamura head of human resources Kubota Masatoshi].

NRSMJ 19 March 2002, Yookadō to Sebunirebun, kanrishoku ni kōbosei [Ito Yokado and Seven Eleven, open recruitment system for management positions].

NRSMJ 25 April 2002, Ōte suupaa, paato, kanrishoku ni sekkyoku tōyō [Part-timers in large supermarkets, progressive use in management positions].

NRSMJ 12 October 2002, Makksubaryu Tōhoku, kōsotsu saiyō wa paato kara [MaxValu Tohoku – fresh high school graduates to be initially employed as part-timers].

NRSMJ 17 October 2002, Rojaasu, dōryō, buka mo kinmu hyōka [Rogers – colleagues and subordinates to be involved in work evaluation].

NRSMJ 23 April 2003, Worumaato ryū, 'itami' mo jojo ni, Seiyū, shain 4 wari gensaku o keikaku [Wal-Mart style, distress increases gradually, plan to reduce Seiyu's employees by 40%].

NRSMJ 25 November 2003, Rainen kara zenshain nenbōsei, Tōkyū Hyakka, taishokukin 25% sage [Tokyu Department Store – From next year on all employees on annual salary system, reduction of retirement allowance by 25%].

NRSMJ 13 January 2004, Koopu Sapporo, 7 nen buri ni seishain saiyō [Coop Sapporo to hire regular employees again for first time after 7 years].

NRSMJ 20 January 2004, 1500 nin gensaku, Seiyū no kage [Seiyu's gamble, reduction of 1,500 people].

NRSMJ 10 February 2004, Marui, seishain 95% tenseki [Marui transfers 95% of its regular employees].

NRSMJ 19 February 2004, Seiyū, taishoku kankoku kaihi no kujū [Seiyu, distress of avoiding the advice to retire].

NRSMJ 11 March 2004, Paato katsuyō inochi zuna [Lifeline for the use of part-time employees].

NRSMJ 4 September 2004, Koopu Sapporo, jinji hyōka seido o dōnyū, nōryokukyū no tōkyū, shōkaku ni hanei [Coop Sapporo has introduced employee evaluation system, will reflect in rank and increases in status in ability based pay component].

Nikkeipb.jp (2004a) *Seika shugi ni yotte shiki teika, utsu ni mo* [Due to the merit-based principles the spirit is sinking, and there is also depression], 5 July 2004, http://www.nikkeibp.jp/wcs/leaf/CID/onair/jp/ques/317629.

Nikkeipb.jp (2004b) *Shintō suru mo kōka o jikkan dekinai seika shugi* [The merit-based principle is spreading but results cannot really hit home], 7 December 2004, http://www.nikkeibp.jp/wcs/leaf/CID/onair/jp/ques/348055.

Nikkeipb.jp (2004c) *20dai no 62.5% ga shikaku o toru tame ni benkyōchū* [62.5% of 20 year olds are studying to receive further qualifications], 21 May 2004, http://nikkeibp.jp/wcs/leaf/CID/onair/jp/ques/308877.

Nikkeipb.jp (2005) *Kyariapuran, 76% ga 'yarigai' o* [Career planning, 76% stress fulfillment], 15 March 2005, http://nikkeibp.jp/wcs/leaf/CID/onair/jp/ques/364785.

Nikkeiren (Nihon Keieisha Dantai Renmei, Japan Employer's Federation) (1995) *Shinjidai no 'Nihonteki keiei'* [Japanese style management for the new era], Tokyo: Nihon Keieisha Dantai Renmei.

Nohara, Hiroatsu (1999) Human resources management in Japanese firms undergoing transition: A hierarchical approach, in *Japanese Management in the Low Growth Era*, Daniel Dirks, Jean-Francois Huchet and Thierry Ribault (eds), Berlin: Springer, pp. 244–262.

Nonaka, Ikujiro and Hirotaka Takeuchi (1995) *The Knowledge-creating Company: How Japanese Companies Create the Dynamics of Innovation*, New York: Oxford University Press.

Ogishi, Yonosuke (2006) Current Japanese employment practices and indus-trial relations: The transformation of permanent employment and seniority-based wage system, *Asian Business & Management*, vol. 5, no. 4, pp. 469–485.

Ogura, Kazuya (2005) International comparison of atypical employment: Differing concepts and realities in industrialized countries, *Japan Labor Review*, vol. 2, no. 2, pp. 5–29.

Ōkubo, Yukio (2005) Waakusu Kenkyūjo wa naze kono kenkyū ni tori kunda no ka [Why the Works Institute has taken up this research], *Works*, no. 69, April–May, pp. 2–4.

Osawa, Mari (2001) People in irregular modes of employment: Are they really not subject to discrimination? *Social Science Japan Journal*, vol. 4, no. 2, pp. 183–199.

PRI (Policy Research Institute – Zaimushō Zaimu Sōken Sōgō Seisaku Kenkyūjo) (2003) *Shinten suru kooporeeto gabanansu kaikaku to Nihon kigyō no saisei* [Progressing corporate governance and the rebuilding of Japanese businesses], June, http://www.mof.go.jp/jouhou/soken/kenkyu.htm.

Pucik, Vladimir and Nina Hatvany (1980) Management practices in Japan: An integrated system focusing on human resources, *Social Analysis*, no. 5/6, pp. 154–225.

RGS (Rōmu Gyōsei Kenkyūjo – Institute of Labor Administration) (2005) *Seika shugi jinji seido no dōnyū kōka to mondaiten* [Results and problematic points in the introduction of merit-oriented human resources manage-ment systems], http://www.rosei.or.jp/press/pdf/200503.pdf.

Rengō Rials (Rengō Sōgō Seikatsu Kaihatsu Kenkyūjo) (2002) Kinrōsha no chingin*shisan keisei no arikata nado ni kan suru chōsa kenkyū hōkokusho (tōkei shiryō hen) [Report on the results of the survey concerning the methods determining the wages and wealth of workers (statistical materials)].

Rengo Soken (1994) *Sarariiman no kigyō kizoku ishiki to shokugyō tenkan nōryoku ni kan suru chōsa hōkokusho* [Report on the survey about the company allegiance of salaried workers and the possibility to change workplaces].

Ribault, Thierry (1999) Flexible employment in Japanese retailing: toward a just-in-time employment management, in *Japanese Management in the Low Growth Era*, Daniel Dirks, Jean-François Huchet and Thierry Ribault (eds), Berlin, Heidelberg, New York: Springer, pp. 295–312.

Rosenblatt, Zehava and Zachary Schaeffer (2000) Ethical problems in downsizing, in *The Organization in Crisis*, Ronald J. Burke and Carry L. Cooper (eds), Oxford: Blackwell, pp. 133–150.

Rōsei Jihō 3 January 2003, Seika shugi no genjō to kadai [Current situation and issues concerning performance based pay systems], no. 3568, pp. 42–62.

Saito, Shōri (2004) *Seimei hoken jigyō no genjō to kadai* [Current problems of the life insurance industry], Kinyū Shingikai Kinyū Bunkakai Dai ni bukai Dai 15 kai giji jidai, 16 January 2004, www.fsa.go.jp/singi/singi_kinyu.base.html.

Sankei Shinbun 24 March 2005, NHK rashiku nai tōron bangumi 4 gatsu 2 ka sutaato [A discussion forum program untypical for NHK will start on April 2].

Satō, Hiroki (2001) Atypical employment: A source of flexible work opportunities, *Social Science Japan Journal*, vol. 4, no. 2, pp. 161–181.

Sato, Hiroki (2003) Use of on-site contract workers in the manufacturing sector and revision of the worker-dispatching law, *Japan Labor Bulletin*, April 1, pp. 7–11.

Sato, Hiroki and Yoshihide Sano (2005) Employment category diversification and personnel management problems, *Japan Labor Review*, vol. 2, no. 2, pp. 30–54.

Satō, Hiroki, Mari Osawa and Charles Weathers (2001) 'Atypical' and 'irregular' labour in contemporary Japan: The authors debate, *Social Science Japan Journal*, vol. 4, no. 2, pp. 219–223.

Sato, Hiroki, Yoshihide Sano and Takuma Kimura (2003) *Dai 1 kai seisan genba ni okeru kōnai ukeoi no katsuyō ni kan suru chōsa* [First survey concerning the use of onsite contractors factory manufacturing], SSJ Data Archive Research Paper Series – SSJDA-24, March 2003, University of Tokyo: Information Center for Social Science Research on Japan, Institute of Social Science.

Sezon Sōgō Kenkyūjo (2000) *Ōte ryōbaiten no POS deeta o riyō shita bukka shizū ni kakaru kenkyū* [Research based on price indices using the POS data of leading mass merchandising stores], Tokyo: Sezon Sōgō Kenkyūjo, http://www.sri-saison.gr.jp/linktoPDF.htm.

Sheldon, Charles D. (1976) Japanese aggression and the emperor, 1931–1941, from contemporary diaries, *Modern Asian Studies*, vol. 10, no. 1, pp. 1–40.

Shibata, Hiromichi (2000) The transformation of the wage and performance appraisal system in a Japanese firm, *International Journal of Human Resource Management*, vol. 11, no. 2, pp. 294–313.

Shozugawa, Yuko (2000) Howaitokaraa no tenshoku shijō o meguro gendai to kadai [Current situation and problems concerning the market for white-collar job changers], *Nissei Kisoken Report*, 7 July 2000.

Sōmuchō Tōkeikyoku (2003) *Heisei 14 nen shūgyō kōzō kihon chōsa, kekka no yōyaku* (Basic survey on the employment structure 2002, outline of results), http://www.stat.go.jp/data/shugyou/2002/kakuhou/youyaku.htm.

Sōmuchō Tōkeikyoku (2005) *Rōdōryoku chōsa shōsai kekka no gaiyō* [Labor force survey detailed results], October to December 2004, 1 March 2005, http://www.stat.go.jp/data/roudou/sokuhou/4hanki/dt/index.htm.

Sōmuchō Tōkeikyoku (2008) *Rōdōryoku chōsa reisai shūkei* (Detailed compilation of Labor Force Survey, 1st Quarter 2008), http://www.stat.go.jp/data/roudou/sokuhou/4hanki/dt/index.htm.

Spreitzer, Gretchen M. and Aneil K. Mishra (2000) An empirical examination of a stress-based framework of survivor responses to downsizing, in *The Organization in Crisis*, Ronald J. Burke and Carry L. Cooper (eds), Oxford: Blackwell, pp. 97–118.

Sugimoto, Yoshio (2003) *An Introduction to Japanese Society*, Cambridge: Cambridge University Press.

Suzuki, Atsuko (1996) *Jinji rōmū ga wakaru jiten* (A dictionary to understand personnel management and labor), Tokyo: Nihon Jitsumu Shuppan-sha.

Tabata, Hirokuni (1998) Community and efficiency in the Japanese firm, *Social Science Japan Journal*, vol. 1, no. 2, pp. 199–215.

Takahashi, Nobuo (2004) *Kyomō seika shugi* [Fallacious performance principles], Tōkyo: Nikkei PBsha.

Tatsumichi, Shingo and Motohiro Morishima (2007) Seikashugi from an employee perspective, *Japan Labor Review*, vol. 4, no. 2, pp. 77–103.

Tempstaff (2005) *Temporary Staffing Services in Japan, presentation materials*, French Chamber of Commerce, 29 March 2005, http://www.ccifj.or.jp/lm/lm257/emploi.pdf.

Thelen, Kathreen and Ikuo Kume (1999) The effects of globalization on labor revisited: Lessons from Germany and Japan, *Politics & Society*, vol. 27, no. 4, December 1999, pp. 475–505.

Tōkyō Shōkō Kaigisho (2002) *Rōdō seisaku ni kan suru ankeeto chōsa kekka – Heisei 14 nendo* [Opinion survey concerning labor policies, 2002], http://www.tokyo-cci.or.jp/kaito/chosa/140611–01.html/.

Tōkyō Shōkō Kaigishō (2000 and 2002) *Rōdō seisaku ni kan suru ankeeto chōsa kekka* [Results of the survey concerning employment policies], http://www.tokyo-cci.or.jp/kaito/chosa/chosa.html.

TSC (Tsūshō Sangyō Daijin Kanbō Tōkei Chōsabu) (different years) *Shōgyō tōkeihyō sangyō hen* [Census of commerce – industrial classification], Tōkyō: Tsūsan Tōkei Kyōkai.

Usui, Chikako and Richard A. Colignon (1996) Corporate restructuring: converging world patterns or societally specific embeddedness? *The Sociological Quarterly*, vol. 37, no. 4, pp. 551–578.

Usuki, Masaharu (2002) Henka shitsutsu aru koyō kankō to atarashii kigyō nenkin seido [Changing employment practices and new corporate pension systems], *Nihon rōdō kenkyū zasshi*, no. 504, pp. 24-35.

Varley, Paul H. (2000) *Japanese Culture*, Honolulu: University of Hawaii Press.

Watanabe, Susumu (2000) The Japan model and the future of employment and wage systems, *International Labour Review*, vol. 139, no. 3, pp. 307–333.

Weather, Charles (2001) Changing white-collar workplaces and female temporary workers in Japan, *Social Science Japan Journal*, vol. 4, no. 2, pp. 201–218.

Weathers, Charles (2004) Temporary workers, women and labour policy-making in Japan, *Japan Forum*, vol. 16, no. 3, pp. 423–447.

Weathers, Charles (2005) In search for strategic partners: Japan's campaign for equal opportunity, *Social Science Japan Journal*, vol. 8, no. 1, pp. 69–89.

Works Institute (2000) *Arubaito no shūrō nado ni kan suru chōsa – furiitaa no ishiki-hatarikata no jittai ni tsuite* [Survey concerning the work and other issues of *arubaito* – about the attitudes and the work situation of freeter], 5 June 2000, Tokyo: Recruit Works Institute.

Works Institute (2001) *Hitenkei koyō rōdōsha chōsa 2001* [Survey of workers in irregular employment], Recruit Works Institute.

Works Institute (2004a) *Posuto seika shugi jidai no jinzai manejimento o kangaeru Works jinzai manejimento chōsa 2003* [Thinking about the personnel management of the post-merit principle era – Works personnel management survey 2003], Recruit Works Institute.

Works Institute (2004b) *Dai 21 kai Waakusu daisotsu kyūjin bairitsu chōsa* (21st survey of the Works Institute concerning the ratio of job seekers and job offers for university graduates), 28 April 2004, http://www.works-i.com/flow/survey/download.html#47.

Works Institute (2004c) *Koyō no gendai 2004* [The current employment situation 2004], September 2004, Recruit Works Institute.

Yamada, Masahiro (2004) *Kibō kakusa shakai* [A society with gaps in aspirations], Tokyo: Chikuma Shobo.

Index

Note: *Italic* page numbers indicate figures and tables.